EDUCATING OUR OWN

".... we must strengthen our foundations, we must educate our own people, not this class or that section, but the universal people, every child of Adam."

These words are taken from a speech made by Dr William Hawkins at the opening ceremony of the Hitchin Working Man's and Mechanic's Institute on 21st December 1835.

EDUCATING OUR OWN

THE MASTERS OF HITCHIN BOYS' BRITISH SCHOOL 1810 TO 1929

Researched, written and produced by (in alphabetical order):
Jacky Birch
Scilla Douglas
Pauline Humphries
Elizabeth Hunter
Rosemary Ransome
Terry Ransome

Foreword by Ricardo-Antonio Lopez-Portillo y Lancaster-Jones
With valued contributions and assistance from -
Fiona Dodwell
Sue Fisher

– and many others; please read our acknowledgements!

A British Schools Museum Publication

A British Schools Museum Publication 2008
Copyright © Hitchin British Schools Trust

ISBN 978-0-9536851-6-5

Design: Chris Murray, Allsortz Ltd
Printed by: G C Print Solutions

Publication of this book has been made possible
by a grant from the Heritage Lottery Fund

Cover photograph: Queen Street, looking north, c1890. The British Schools can be seen centre background (Latchmore photograph, Hitchin Museum)

Inside front cover: Extract from the Ordnance Survey map of 1851, showing the Dead Street School (Hitchin Museum)

Half title page: Line drawing adapted from The Royal School Series, Highroads of Geography Book II, 1919

Frontispiece: Queen Street, looking north
Top – c1890 (Latchmore photograph, Hitchin Museum)
Bottom – 2007 (Colin Hewett, Hitchin Camera Club)

Inside back cover: Queen Street from Mr Fitch's gate, looking south towards Hitchin Hill
Top – c1890 (Latchmore photograph, Hitchin Museum)
Bottom – 2007 (Colin Hewett, Hitchin Camera Club)

Back cover: A portrait of Mr Fitch standing by the gate to the Master's house – possibly taken to mark his retirement in 1899 (Hitchin Museum)

Contents

Dedication

While researching the material for this book, we came to appreciate the tremendous efforts made by masters, teachers, trustees and the many others who were associated with the Hitchin British Schools for the first hundred years.

It was never easy to run a school. The stress of the job certainly affected some of our masters; but we can see the positive results of their perseverance. This book is dedicated to their memory.

The uniqueness and value of this historic educational site was first identified in the 1970s by Mrs Jill Grey. When she succeeded in getting the buildings 'listed' as a heritage site, the first steps were taken to preserve them. Efforts to save them were intensified when the current Hitchin British Schools Trust was founded in 1990 by Brian Limbrick, Elizabeth Hunter and Robert Dimsdale, with Fiona Dodwell taking on the role of Trust Secretary in the early days.

In 1994, the Trust took possession of the British Schools, and a new era began. Hundreds of volunteers joined in. As with the early masters, their work was fraught with problems, but hard work and commitment produced results. The buildings on the site, where the masters lived and taught, still fulfil their original purpose – education and learning. This book is dedicated to everyone who has supported this project.

Finally, we do not forget the thousands of children who came here. A visitor to the British Schools Museum can sit quietly in one of the classrooms, or gaze over the empty playground and let the imagination flow; the school will fill with children. This is for them, too.

The British Schools Museum, Hitchin 2006.

Foreword

by Ricardo-Antonio Lopez-Portillo y Lancaster-Jones

"All who have meditated on the art of governing mankind have been convinced that the fate of empires depends on the education of youth."
Aristotle (384 BC – 322 BC)

Firstly, I thank the cordial invitation of Terry Ransome, a Trustee of the Hitchin British Schools Museum, to write the foreword to this book. I feel especially honoured, for in my case there's an exceptional relationship with the Hitchin British Schools as I'm a descendant of the educationalist Joseph Lancaster – my great-great-great-great-grandfather.

The year 2008 commemorates the 200th anniversary of a visit to Hitchin by Lancaster.

Joseph Lancaster (1778-1838), who created the Lancasterian System of education, visited Hitchin in 1808 and met with Samuel Whitbread and, amongst others, William Wilshere, who in 1810 opened the first Lancasterian School in Hertfordshire, precisely in Hitchin.

World leaders like George III in Great Britain, James Monroe in the USA, Tsar Alexander I in Russia, Simon Bolivar in Great Colombia, and Ferdinand VII in Spain, all adopted the Lancasterian System of education. The system was used in almost all countries of the world.

The Marquis de La Fayette (1757-1834) said in the Legislative Chamber of France: *"Now, gentlemen, the Lancasterian System is, since the invention of printing, the greatest step which has been made for the extension of prompt, easy and popular instruction".*

The Duke of La Rochefoucauld-Liancourt (1747-1827) translated and published one of Lancaster's works under the name of *Système Anglais d'Instruction*, reorganizing the schools of France.

Simon Bolivar (1783-1830) met Joseph Lancaster in London and learned about his educational system. When Bolivar led his country to independence, he invited Joseph Lancaster to go to Caracas to develop his system there.

While Lancaster and his family were in Caracas in 1824, he had

Ricardo-Antonio and Francisco-Xavier Lopez-Portillo y Lancaster-Jones with the High Sheriff of Hertfordshire, the Hon. Richard Pleydell-Bouverie, reopening the Lancasterian Schoolroom watched by Brian Limbrick.

interviews with Mexican diplomats and was told of the Lancasterian Company founded in Mexico two years earlier.

Lancaster and Basarde (an official at the Mexican embassy) convinced Richard M Jones (married to Joseph Lancaster's only daughter Elizabeth) to go to Mexico City and impart his knowledge and experience of the Lancasterian System to schools in the town. Richard and Elizabeth arrived there in September 1825.

I've been privileged, for along with my brothers Rodrigo-Alonso and Francisco-Xavier, I grew up with the knowledge of my ancestry, thanks to my parents Armando Lopez-Portillo y Garcia-Rojas and Luz Isabel Lancaster-Jones y Padilla (d.1981).

Everything about my ancestor and his system of education has always been of interest: articles, letters, documents, expositions… and of course books, like *Joseph Lancaster, the Poor Child's Friend: Educating the Poor in the Early Nineteenth Century,* by Joyce Taylor.

To celebrate the bicentenary of Bolivar's birth, Sir Edgar Vaughan, at the time British Ambassador to Venezuela, published in two volumes *Joseph Lancaster en Caracas y sus relaciones con El Libertador Simon Bolivar* (1987). Sir Edgar had been in touch with my grandfather, Ricardo Lancaster-Jones (d.1983). I was fortunate to be able to stay in contact with him during the last period of his life and, seeing my interest in the subject, he put me in touch with Mora Dickson, author of the book *Teacher Extraordinary. Joseph Lancaster*, who became a good friend, almost one of the family.

Through the kind generosity of John and Janet Lancaster, we received the warmest invitation to London to participate in the July 1998 celebrations of the bicentenary of the opening of Lancaster's first school for poor children in Kent Street, Southwark in 1798, followed by the reopening of the Lancasterian Schoolroom at Hitchin's British Schools Museum.

I was allowed to extend an invitation to the then Ambassador of Mexico to the United Kingdom, His Excellency Santiago Oñate Laborde, as the Lancasterian Schools had been a fundamental part of the education in independent Mexico since before 1826. Also, Joseph Lancaster's grandson, Alfonso Lancaster-Jones (b. 1841), was appointed by the Mexican President as Extraordinary Envoy for the Coronation of Edward VII and held the same post as Ambassador and Full Powered Minister to the United Kingdom.

It was a significant honour for my brother Francisco-Xavier and me to be asked to cut the inaugural ribbon, alongside the Hon. Richard Pleydell-Bouverie, High Sheriff of Hertfordshire, and to participate and be witness to the continuity and preservation of the work and memory of Joseph Lancaster.

Since then, this cause has continued to be supported by more hard working, benevolent people of Hitchin. Surely Joseph Lancaster would be very proud of this wonderful team.

Mexico City, 2008

Introduction

The house at number 42 Queen Street, Hitchin was always known as 'Mr Fitch's'. Not surprisingly, for William John Fitch lived there for 45 years until his death in 1902. Mr Fitch was Master of the Boys' British School from 1854 to 1899. He saw the house built in 1857 and was the only master to ever live there. A blue plaque to commemorate Mr Fitch was unveiled in 2004.

The blue plaque on Mr Fitch's house.

The Hitchin British Schools Trust took over the old school buildings, including the Headmaster's house, in 1994 and opened a museum there in 1996. Guided tours in the early days of the British Schools Museum told visitors of the history of elementary education across the country; how Joseph Lancaster set up monitorial schools, how the National Schools were formed in response, and how the British government was persuaded to embrace education for all.

Ever present, though, was a local story – the story of one man, William John Fitch, who, as Reginald Hine asserts in *Hitchin Worthies*, saw 3,333 pupils pass by his front door on their way into school over a period of 45 years.

That story was never written. Information had been gleaned from archives and, indeed, from two of W J Fitch's great-granddaughters who joined the museum's volunteer team. There are books to be found in the museum's shop describing the history of the highly important school buildings, as well as what life in the school was like in Victorian times. But nothing has been published on the life and times of W J Fitch, or of the other masters who lived and worked here.

However, 2007 would see the 150th anniversary of Mr Fitch moving in to the Master's house. So when the Trust learnt of a Local Heritage Initiative offering funding for volunteer-led projects to celebrate local history, an application was made to them to finance a project focussing on the history of the school and the masters who ran it – in particular Mr W J Fitch.

The Hitchin British Schools Trust was fortunate and grateful to receive such funding – awarded and managed by the Heritage Lottery Fund. This publication is part of that project and was very much a team effort.

I congratulate the team for their professionalism in researching and producing this excellent book, which I am sure will be enjoyed by many.

Fiona Dodwell, Curator

Room for Improvement

EDUCATION IN HITCHIN IN THE 18TH CENTURY

A visit to the town of Hitchin, Hertfordshire, in the 18th and early 19th century is essential to understanding the importance of William Wilshere's legacy – his School of 1810.

Hitchin was a small country market town with an economy driven by the corn trade, malting and brewing. It was home to coaching inns, banks, shops and a wide variety of skilled craftsmen. In 1801 it boasted a population of a little over 3,000, comparable in size to today's nearby village of Codicote. It was a town in which people would have recognised many of their neighbours, by face if not by name. Even before the railway age, Hitchin had been a hub of transport, and its relative proximity to London meant that it was not entirely closed to ideas or progress.

Hitchin was remarkably free of the influence of big County families, all the energy and enterprise was generated by those who made their living in the vicinity, in trade or the professions. This group were behind all the public and charitable schemes which evolved at the beginning of the 19th century. Most of these men (and they were 'men', but backed up in many cases by energetic and supportive women) were Nonconformists. Although, numerically, Anglicans were probably in the majority locally, the 18th century Church of England was rather 'in the doldrums', with the notable exception of one Hitchin vicar.

At the end of the 17th century, as a result of the Toleration Act passed in

1689, Nonconformists, who had long been present in the town, were free to build their own meeting houses. Probably the most influential (and certainly the wealthiest) of these groups were the Quakers. The Independents had their meeting house in Dead Street, now Queen Street, on the site of today's Wilshere Court next door to the British Schools. Their congregation included many influential families, such as the Wilsheres who had originally been farmers and maltsters.

William Wilshere (1754–1824) is a hero of our story. The Baptists, who had many tradesmen and maltsters amongst their flock, tended to 'plough

their own furrow' as far as public works were concerned. However in Hitchin at this time there was remarkable co-operation between different religious groups. Fertile ground for progress.

And in education, progress was certainly needed.

Pegasus Retirement Homes recognised the importance of the Wilshere family to Hitchin when they named their development in Queen Street, 2006.

Only a small proportion of children would have received any education at all. Some would have been with 'child-minders', women who for a few pennies kept them out of mischief until they could become economically active. Others might have been regarded as an investment opportunity and been sent for a small sum to a Plait School, to learn skills which would contribute to the family budget. In 1804, the agricultural expert Arthur Young noted that Hertfordshire women could earn £1 a week by plaiting straw for the hat trade; almost twice a farm worker's wage.

But there were schools in the town, and Hitchin contained excellent examples of both an Endowed Grammar School and a Girls' Charity School, plus a sprinkling of private schools and academies. We also know that Dame Schools existed for younger children, probably of varying quality, some being simply child-minding establishments.

Hitchin's Endowed Grammar School probably had its origins in the school set up by Ralph Radcliffe in the Priory following the Dissolution of the Monasteries. It later moved to premises in Tilehouse Street, to a house taken over by the Free School in 1639. In that year John Mattocke left the revenue of three acres of land to support an *"able and learned schoolmaster"* to instruct Hitchin children in *"good literature and virtuous education for the avoidance of idleness, the mother of all vice and wickedness"*. In time other endowments were made, poor children being the object of the bequests.

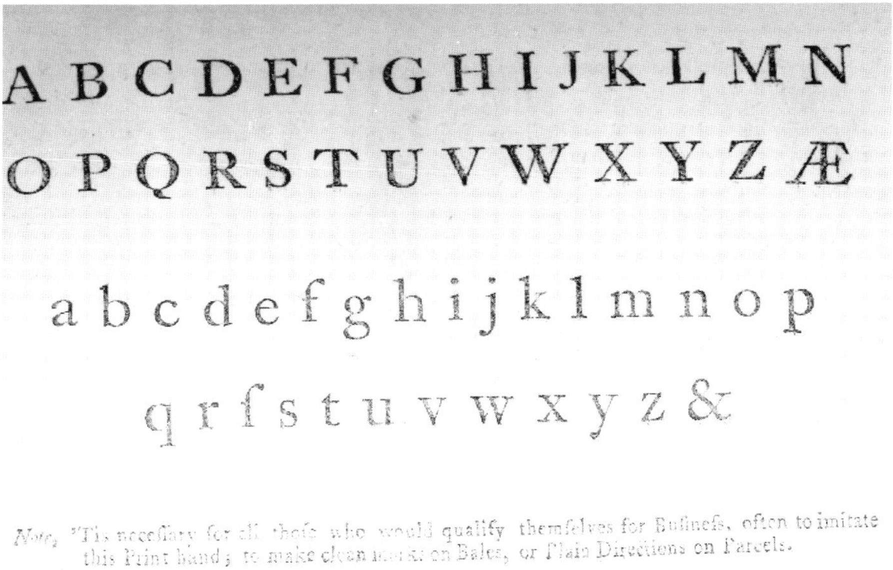

A B C D E F G H I J K L M N

O P Q R S T U V W X Y Z Æ

a b c d e f g h i j k l m n o p

q r f s t u v w x y z &

Note, 'Tis neceffary for all thofe who would qualify themfelves for Bufinefs, often to imitate this Print hand; to make clean marks on Bales, or Plain Directions on Parcels.

An extract from 'The Instructor or Young Man's Best Companion' by George Fisher, 1794

Originally, Latin was not taught, and there was an emphasis on English and Arithmetic, thought fitting for boys whose future lay in trade. The footnote on the bottom of the page from *The Instructor or Young Man's Best Companion*, emphasises this – *"Note, 'Tis necessary for all those who would qualify themselves for Business, often to imitate this Print hand; to make clean marks on Bales, or Plain Directions on Parcels".*

While elsewhere in the county many similar schools declined as the value of their endowments lessened, Hitchin's Free School flourished, albeit with a few hiccoughs here and there. Reference to its Trustees' Minute Book shows that parental occupations remained predominantly artisan during the 18th century.

The Free School catered only for boys. But in 1719, Dame Mary Radcliffe, inspired by the Charity School movement which swept the country in the early 18th century, began a fund *"for teaching and clothing poor girls of Hitchin"*, which was augmented by subscriptions and *"collections made at the Church Doors"*. Later endowments followed. Girls were normally aged between ten and thirteen on admission and were to be taught *"nothing but what shall be consistent for the station they are most probably designed for, besides their Reading and being Catechised …sewing, knitting, spinning, mending their clothes and such like"*.

Hitchin's Charity School was one of the many founded in the early 18th century. It was an expression of middle-class conscience, but there was no desire to raise the poor above their perceived station in life. The aim of these schools was to inculcate sound morality, work habits and a desire to please.

❏ ❏ ❏ ❏ ❏

For those higher up the social scale, educational opportunities increased. Because Hitchin was a busy market town and a focus of neighbouring communities, it was able to draw fee-paying pupils to a variety of small private Grammar Schools. These would have accepted boarding pupils, and given the classical education so dear to the middle-classes. A succession of Reverend gentlemen ran schools in the town, or took in house boarders in order to augment their incomes.

One such gentleman was the Reverend John Dyer who ran an academy in Tilehouse Street from 1795 until 1819. It was patronised by wealthy local families, and lives on in the excellent description given by a former pupil, William Lucas, the Diarist and Quaker brewer. Dyer's was considered *"a first rate concern in those days ...many of the little gentry, clergy and principal farmers sent their sons to it"*. Dyer was a good example of many masters of the time. *"He was truly a man of few words but many blows ...I should not be doing my duty to your parents if I passed such conduct by unpunished. Hold out your hand, you infamous brat"*. Dyer's classes were obviously managed by an usher, as one was dismissed for hitting William with a ruler.

Hitchin Quakers at this time expressed their educational concern by supporting the establishment of a Quaker school in Yorkshire. Ackworth was founded in 1779, and Hitchin Meeting made a generous donation of £182, followed up by an annual subscription of eight guineas. This entitled them to place one local pupil, free of charge to the parents, presumably Friends who had fallen on hard times. A private Quaker school did exist in the town between 1789 and 1801, run by George Blaxland, and appears to have been of good repute, as it was patronised by prominent local families, but no details remain.

Elementary education of a sort was available but only for families able to afford fees. Again William Lucas gave a graphic description of his youthful experiences in his journal, and although the era was slightly later, conditions were probably very similar in the 18th century. Young William, son of a prosperous and cultured middle-class family, was sent to a Dame School in Church Yard, kept by a tailor's wife *"a fat vulgar-looking woman who with a long stick could reach the most remote of her pupils and which was sometimes employed to poke out the sparrow's nests from under eaves, kept order in a low cottage room in a cottage first floor"*. Lucas had no recollection of being taught anything and was later sent to an academy in Bucklersbury *"where John Read, his wife and two daughters kept a numerous school, the greater part girls"*. Again, application was enforced by use of *"a hairbrush with a wiry back ... which used to make our hands tingle very frequently"*. If this quality of tuition was the best available to the wealthy middle-class of the town, that provided by similar unrecorded little schools was probably inferior.

But change was afoot. The years from 1750 onwards had seen a rapid change in social and economic conditions, as the country moved from the old rural-based economy of the past to its industrial future. Hitchin's population more than doubled in the first half of the 19th century as families left the land and sought to join the town economy. Although Hertfordshire did not experience the evils of the factory system, where children were exploited by parents and employers, it was close enough to London to be influenced by the humanitarian concerns that were being expressed.

The Sunday School movement had begun in 1780, when Robert Raikes took children running wild in the streets of Gloucester and tempted them to acquire the rudiments of Scripture and reading by a system of rewards. In his book *Market Town*, Tony Foster cites 1787 as the earliest reference to

BACK STREET SUNDAY SCHOOL, 1803

Taken from a painting found many years ago in the Hitchin Congregational Church safe. The painting was by an unknown hand and we do not know who produced the illustration. It appears in R Hine's book 'The History of Hitchin' Vol II, 1929.

Hitchin Sunday Schools, when William Lucas paid five guineas towards *"an establishment of those so called Sunday Schools in the town"*. The Minute Books of Queen Street Congregational Church record a school started in 1803 by the Independent Chapel in Back Street, led by the Pastor's wife, Mrs Williams.

The Minute Books also record an earlier school *"set up by Miss Wilshere and her brother in a cottage previous to this date"*. Although there is evidence of Anglican involvement by the Reverend Mark Hildesley in the teaching of the Catechism to young children in the 18th century, their Sunday School is of a slightly later date and used rooms in Barnard's Yard, Dead Street. The Baptists established a thriving school in 1812, at their Tilehouse Street Chapel. By 1814 it had an average attendance of 130 with both morning and afternoon sessions and a Church service to follow. Much of the time was spent on the rudiments of reading. In 1815, the first Sunday School treat was enjoyed, plum cake and ale *"on the hill"*. A great deal of social work obviously took place, with visits to sick children and rewards for good attendees – vouchers for hats (boys) and stockings (girls).

A start had been made in education, and William Wilshere as a Christian businessman and lawyer, supported the aims of this new movement. Sunday Schools uncovered not only the real ignorance of poor children, but also their desire and ability to learn to read. They also acted as an important moral and disciplinary tool for children and were for many their only opportunity to acquire any education at all.

So in the field of education, by the early 19th century, Hitchin had some undeniable assets. It was home to a co-operative and influential middle-class, steeped in Nonconformist philanthropy but also with the energy and contacts to promote change. They were backed up by an army of well-intentioned but far from wealthy townsfolk who provided a continuous source of funding and hard work. This enabled people to work towards a common goal.

Researched and written by Pauline Humphries

chapter

2

Of Monitors and Masters

ELEMENTARY EDUCATION FOR ALL

In general, the state of education in Hitchin reflected the national situation. As the 18th Century became the early 19th, life for a poor child was harsh and without hope. Many were put to work labouring in factories, mines or on farms from a young age. Some parents, in despair and poverty, mistreated or ignored their children. In the larger cities, unruly behaviour from gangs of boys was a real social problem. Very few children had any kind of education.

Some parents who could afford a few pence might send their offspring to Dame Schools, usually run by women doing little more than childminding, with young children crammed into a living room or small hall.

The Church had schools; there were Charity Schools, Sunday Schools and Ragged Schools – for those who literally had no shoes – but for the vast majority of children, particularly girls, reading and writing were mysteries they would never unravel. That suited many people too, who felt the poor should be kept in their rightful place, serving their betters.

But some citizens did have other ideas. In Adam Smith's influential 1776 work *The Wealth of Nations*, he argued that the poor should be educated so that they would become more orderly, have self respect and not be swayed by militants.

In 1807 Samuel Whitbread MP proposed free education for the poor. His Parochial Schools Bill was defeated after fierce debate but the belief that education was a good thing for all was gaining ground.

In addition, the many factories and businesses that had sprung up across the country as a result of the industrial revolution were demanding a more literate workforce – to read instructions, count and measure goods, and above all to write things down. The need was growing for elementary education for all.

One man played a large part in making the change happen. He was Joseph Lancaster, born on 25th November 1778, in Kent Street, Southwark, London. He was the youngest of ten children born to Richard and Sarah Lancaster. Richard was an ex-soldier and owner of a small business making and selling cane sieves.

Joseph Lancaster was a contradictory, charismatic, infuriating, driven man with a vision of childhood quite at variance with his times – he saw the poor and ignorant all around him and wanted to help. This unlikely hero managed to change and improve the lives of countless children by giving them a chance to learn.

At the age of 12 or so, Lancaster started work in his father's business and with his wages soon began buying and selling books. It was around this time that he became a Quaker. According to William Corston, a contemporary of Lancaster, he 'ran away' to Bristol at the age of 14 and signed up as a volunteer aboard a ship. He intended to journey to Jamaica *"to teach the poor blacks the word of God"*, but was sent to Milford Haven instead. After three weeks, he wrote a letter to his mother, which enabled her to find him and arrange his return home.

The Lancasterian System – Reading being taught by monitors at draft stations.

LANCASTER SETS UP SCHOOL

When Lancaster returned home he became an assistant to a local teacher in a common day school, moving on to become an assistant teacher in a boarding school for the children of the Society of Friends at Colne in Essex.

In 1798 he opened his own school in a room of his father's house in Kent Street (now Tabard Street) – not far from Borough Road. He taught children the three R's.

His school quickly grew, so he moved first into one of his father's workrooms and then into a large workshop in the Borough Road itself. There he charged his pupils four pence a week, but if the parents could not afford to pay he would educate the child for nothing.

His school was a great success; in the autumn of 1799 he moved again, to a large building just off the Borough Road. A handbill appeared in 1800 on the streets of Southwark proclaiming *"Education on a liberal plan, at The Academy, No 1 James Street, near the Borough Road, Southwark….. Writing books are sold at very low prices, and the use of Bibles, Grammars, Slates, Pens and Ink are found gratis"*.

James Street is now known as King James Street. This was the school Lancaster described in his first edition of *Improvements in Education* in 1803 – *"wherein near Three Hundred Children are educated, and trained to habits conducive to the Welfare of Society"*.

As numbers increased, however, Lancaster found it more and more difficult to teach all the children himself and yet he could not afford the

wages for an assistant teacher. His solution was to get the more able pupils (called 'monitors') to help.

But how did the 'Monitorial System' work? How could one master teach so many children in one school?

Lancaster had found an answer. He knew that Dr Andrew Bell in Madras, India, had developed the 'mutual system of instruction' – the master taught the older, more able pupils who in turn passed on their knowledge to the others. Large numbers of children could thus be educated for very little cost.

Lancaster developed the concept further. He perfected a system in which one book could serve the needs of a schoolroom of 300 boys. Printed pages could be pasted on boards to hang around the walls. Each monitor would lead nine or ten boys to a 'draft station' at the wall, to stand around a semicircle drawn on the floor. The boys would learn from the appropriate lesson board hung on the wall in front of them.

Lancaster had to keep costs as low as possible, so he had beginners practise their letters and numbers by writing in sand, only progressing to slates when they were considered adept enough.

He also had to work hard to encourage his pupils to remain at school. He did this by developing a system of rewards. Reward tokens were given for meritorious work. They could be exchanged for a coveted prize – a hoop, ball or kite – kept temptingly in full view of the scholars, hanging from the ceiling of the schoolroom.

Monitors wore large silver badges. There were monitors of order, slate monitors and, of course, teaching monitors. Each monitor received a small annual payment for his services. How proud they would be! How younger pupils would aspire to such a position!

As a Quaker, Lancaster opposed the almost universal use of corporal punishment. For the inevitable instances of bad work or misbehaviour, he devised ways of shaming or ridiculing his boys. Those who could not read their letters or numbers would remain at the lower end of a draft station, moving up only when they had learned their lesson. Bad behaviour would result in a label being hung around a boy's neck, telling of his misdeed.

Lancaster logically argued that his monitorial system was in theory capable of teaching 1,000 boys at a time with one master. Indeed, a list of schools compiled by the British and Foreign School Society in 1897 included a number capable of accommodating more than 1,000 – several even able to accommodate up to 1,600 pupils. We are unable to verify, however, if such numbers were actually taught at the same time in one schoolroom.

The system was certainly economical and it worked, and it soon began to spread across the country. Lancaster always welcomed visitors into his schoolroom to see his system in action; they would be encouraged to make subscriptions to further his work. Wealthy and generous benefactors included (from 1801) Henry Thornton the MP for Southwark, Zachary Macaulay and William Wilberforce.

In 1804 Lancaster married Elizabeth Bonner. In the autumn of that year he was presented to King George III at Windsor. In 1805 Lancaster went to see the King again, in Weymouth, and presented him with specially bound copies of *Improvements in Education*. On this occasion the King expressed his wish that every child in his kingdom should be able to read the Bible and agreed to subscribe £100 annually. He also commanded Queen Charlotte and the five princesses to subscribe. They were prestigious benefactors indeed, and were joined by the nobility including the Duke of Bedford.

But although Lancaster was a visionary and an excellent teacher, he was from a humble background, without his own financial resources and lacking the ability to manage the funds he was able to raise.

Demands on his income were many and varied. He had to maintain not only his wife Elizabeth and their only child Betsy, but also his school and even a printing press and a slate-making workshop he had set up next door. He had started a library of books for his boys; he even began providing mid-day meals for needy children. His only sources of income were his pupils' fees and donations from supporters, so it is not surprising that he was frequently in debt.

When the school received Royal patronage, Lancaster thought that his money worries were over. Indeed he even renamed his school 'The Royal Free School' and dispensed with pupils' fees.

In early 1807 Lancaster was detained in a 'sponging house', with the threat of being thrown into debtors' prison, until notable members of the Quaker community paid off his debts and took a working interest in his venture. William Corston, Joseph Fox and William Allen were among them. In 1808 they founded the 'Royal Lancasterian Institution for the Education of the Poor'. Their aim was to put Lancaster's cause on a firm foundation, and to avoid future financial problems.

⌐ ⌐ ⌐ ⌐ ⌐

Lancaster had to endure intense religious pressures as well as his money problems. His schools were strictly non-denominational, and that brought him into conflict with the Church of England.

The Church wanted children to be educated, if indeed they had to be educated at all, as Anglicans, mainly so they could read the Bible, but little else. The Church's advocate, Mrs Sarah Trimmer, was afraid that Lancaster's system, based on merit not class, would make the poor *"aspire to be nobles of the land and to take the place of the hereditary nobility".* Among her many supporters were the poets Wordsworth and Coleridge, contributing to a controversy that ran deep.

Mrs Trimmer mounted a largely successful campaign to blacken Lancaster's name, claiming he had stolen his ideas from Dr Andrew Bell.

There were important differences in the two men's approach and Bell's emphasis on keeping the poor in their place appealed to the Anglicans. *"In Utopian schemes for the universal diffusion of general knowledge, there is a risk of elevating those who are doomed to the drudgery of daily labour above their station and rendering them unhappy and discontented with their lot",* he said.

But the Church of England eventually gave in, and in 1811 founded The National Society for the Education of the Labouring Poor. Their schools were to be known as National Schools – the forerunners of today's Church of England Schools – and Dr Bell was brought out of retirement to be the Superintendent. And for the next ninety years, the two systems – the National and the British – took in and educated young boys and girls across the country. They stayed in school for as long as their parents could afford their pennies, or until paid work beckoned.

THE BRITISH AND FOREIGN SCHOOL SOCIETY TAKES OVER

In 1814, only six years after it was founded, the Royal Lancasterian Institution found itself at odds with Lancaster. Against the will of his trustees, Lancaster had set up a middle-class boarding school in Tooting for his own profit, but it resulted in his second bankruptcy. Lancaster's affairs were therefore very firmly taken over by the trustees and the Royal Lancasterian Institution became the British and Foreign School Society (generally abbreviated to BFSS). Lancaster became a paid Superintendent but had no part in the management of the society.

In 1817 a fundraising effort by William Allen and Joseph Fox resulted in a new building on the Borough Road site. 500 boys and 300 girls were taught in separate schoolrooms either side of the large main building. It was now also well established as a training college for teachers.

The school was regularly visited by the nobility and foreign visitors, including Simon Bolivar who was to become liberator of South America. Tsar Alexander I of Russia visited in 1812. Lancaster's system of instruction was being introduced across the world – not just to educate children but even the Tsar's army. The King of Spain supported Lancasterian schools, and in 1815 the 'Society of Elementary Schools' was founded in France based on Lancasterian principles.

The Interior of the Royal Free School, Borough Road.

Lancaster's Royal Free School with rewards hanging in full view of the scholars.

13

> *Sarah Trimmer's and Dr Bell's sentiments were reflected perfectly, even as late as 1848, in the last verse (now conveniently omitted from hymn books) of 'All Things Bright and Beautiful':*
>
> *The rich man in his castle,*
> *The poor man at his gate,*
> *God made them, high or lowly,*
> *And order'd their estate.*
>
> *Cecil Francis Alexander, 1848*

THE GOVERNMENT TAKES AN INTEREST

We have not yet talked of the Government's involvement in education. That is because so far there had been no involvement. Things only began to change following the Reform Bill of 1832, which brought pressure for social reform, including pleas for the creation of a national system of education. The Roebuck Bill of 1833 marked a very important milestone.

There were some familiar arguments in Parliament from detractors – Joseph Hume objected that there was not enough funding proposed to establish a national system; William Cobbett claimed that education was not improving the condition of the country, pointing out that the increase in educational facilities had been accompanied by an increase in crime. It was even said that there was now a new race of idlers – the schoolmasters and schoolmistresses.

But Mr W A Roebuck's Bill was passed, resulting in the first government grant for education – £20,000 – being issued *"...in aid of Private Subscriptions for the Erection of School Houses, for the Education of the Poorer Classes in Great Britain ...."* The amount was divided equally between the National Society and the British and Foreign School Society. Every grant made to schools and paid out by the Societies had to be matched by an equal amount of funding, raised locally.

In 1846, the Government acted again, this time to support the training of teachers. In the Lancasterian system, the monitors only remained in school as long as they were boys and still learning. Employment would eventually take them away, and the master would have to start all over again training new monitors.

Under the new system, boys of the age of 13 or so could, if they had achieved the required standards, be apprenticed to the master for five years

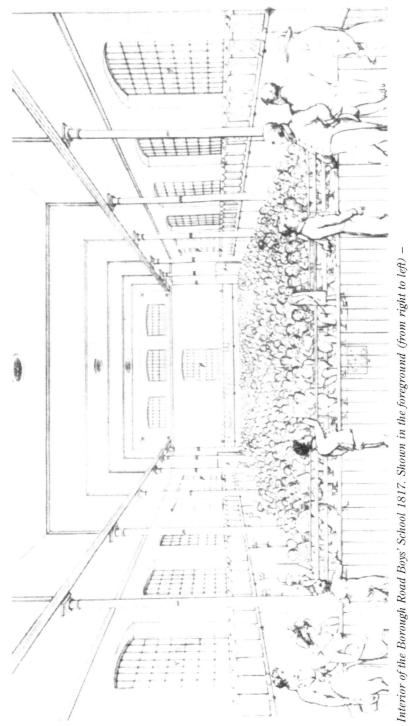

Interior of the Borough Road Boys' School 1817. Shown in the foreground (from right to left) – William Allen, the Dukes of Sussex and Kent, the master John Pickton, the black monitor-general William Jagon who later became master of a school in the West Indies, and on the left a visiting family.

to learn the trade of teacher. They would be paid a small wage funded by the Government. At the end of their time, they could apply for a Queen's Scholarship to enter a teacher training college.

This system, known as the Pupil Teacher System, was one result of many initiatives and experiments in education by a Select Committee of the Privy Council, formed in 1839. Dr James Kay, later Sir James Kay-Shuttleworth, was secretary, and is credited with developing and introducing the new system.

❏ ❏ ❏ ❏ ❏

So, over time, the need for education of the less privileged classes that Lancaster had highlighted was finally recognised at the highest level. The Government was involved – with budgets, committees and resources all focussed on education. One of the victims of the changes was the Lancasterian system itself, which became old-fashioned and fell out of use – earlier in the United Kingdom than overseas. Great schoolrooms around the country, and indeed the world, were divided, demolished or replaced by smaller classrooms. The pupil teachers needed smaller rooms in which to practise their craft.

Yet still it was the British and the National Schools that performed the lion's share of the work of educating the lower classes. They ran separately and peacefully alongside one another until W E Forster's Education Act of 1870 finally determined that elementary education was to be available for all children aged 5 to 10. The Act permitted the setting up of schools, to be run by School Boards, in all communities where there were insufficient numbers of voluntary school places. It was again no easy passage; the Church attacked the non-denominational nature of the proposals, others were against them on grounds of cost. The new schools were to be known as Board Schools and would operate alongside both the National and British Schools. Even then, education was not compulsory – that was not introduced until Mr Mundella's Act of 1880.

However, elementary education was not yet free. The School Boards could charge for attendance, but the 1870 Act had at least limited charges to 9d per week. In 1891, when the Government made grants available to schools to enable them to cease charging, parents gained the right to demand free education for their children. It is perhaps not surprising that the majority of schools had to comply!

In the early days of the 20th century came the government action that would bring an end to both the independence of the British Schools movement and the School Boards. The 1902 Balfour-Morant Act brought education under municipal control – the county councils and borough councils became the new Local Education Authorities. In all, some 2,500 School Boards and 800 School Attendance Committees were replaced by just 300 new local authorities, most of which still exist today.

Nowhere is the development of elementary education reflected more completely than in the British Schools in Hitchin. The whole history of the site echoes the numerous significant changes made over a period of nearly 100 years. Between them, the masters of the Boys' School saw it all. Lancasterian monitors were replaced by pupil teachers and then assistant masters. Finally, in the opening years of the 20th century, the British Schools were taken over by Hertfordshire County Council; the end of one era, but the beginning of another.

WHAT BECAME OF LANCASTER?

When the Royal Lancasterian Institution was formed in 1808, Lancaster was relieved of his immediate financial pressures. He was able to travel the country explaining how the three Rs could be taught efficiently, economically and constructively, and all the time trying to raise funds. It was one of these tours that took him to Hitchin in 1808.

Meanwhile, Lancaster's school system had been taken to many parts of the world. Joseph continued his drive to spread the word and, funded by his supporters, went to New York in 1818. He arrived on 24th August, with his wife Elizabeth and his twelve-year-old daughter, young Elizabeth (Betsy), and one of his young teachers, Richard Jones.

The first Lancasterian school on *Joseph Lancaster by John Hazlitt, c1818* the American continent had been established in New York in 1806. By 1815 the third had been opened there. The first school in Canada, in Halifax, Nova Scotia opened the same year.

Lancaster was befriended by the Governor of New York, DeWitt Clinton, but by 1819 he had moved to Washington where he was received by President Monroe and permitted to address Congress on two occasions.

Sadly his wife Elizabeth died a year later. Then, in 1824, his daughter Elizabeth and teacher Richard Jones married.

Joseph travelled widely in the Americas, spending time in Caracas (then a city in Colombia, but now capital of Venezuela) and returning to New Jersey and Montreal, before finally settling in Philadelphia. Lancasterian schools opened in Boston, Baltimore, Philadelphia and Washington. In New York the 'Society of Public Schools' encompassed sixty schools.

Lancaster was never to return to England. In 1838, aged 59, on a visit to New York, he fell under the wheels of a horse-drawn waggon and died the next day. He was buried in Houston Street Cemetery, Brooklyn but in 1874 the last remains from that cemetery, including those of Lancaster, were moved and re-interred in Greenwood Cemetery, Prospect Park, New York.

Lancaster died a frustrated and bitter man. His memoirs are a long rambling tome, describing unfulfilled hopes and dreams. But although he suffered much personal failure, his passion was taken up by many across the world who introduced his systems and made them work – providing 'Education for All' around the globe.

Researched and written by Sue Fisher and Terry Ransome

chapter

3

From Malthouse to Schoolroom

SETTING UP THE SCHOOL IN HITCHIN

William Wilshere (1754–1824) was the eldest son of William and Susanna Wilshere of Hitchin. After William there were fourteen more children, among them John, Thomas and Sarah. Young William was educated at the old Free School at the top of Tilehouse Street in Hitchin. The curriculum at the old Free School of reading, writing and the 'casting of accounts' gave him useful knowledge for his future career as a lawyer and landowner.

William senior was a farmer and maltster, but did not prosper and so was glad to find employment in Richard Tristram's legal practice in Portmill Lane, Hitchin. Young William followed in his father's footsteps and was articled as a clerk in Tristram's firm, whose business included many lucrative stewardships of estates around Hitchin.

1785 was quite a year for Wilshere. At the age of 31 he married Martha Wortham of Royston. In the same year he inherited the whole of Tristram's practice. Wilshere later acquired the lease of the Royal Manor of Hitchin.

Sadly, Martha died on 18th September 1786, after only 13 months of married life. They had no children, and William did not marry again (but he later adopted his nephew, also named William (1804–1867), the eldest son of his brother Thomas).

William Wilshere was a businessman. Understanding the need for accessible and secure finances, he joined three other Hitchin men – J Pierson, H Crabb and D Chapman – and became a partner in the new Hitchin and Hertfordshire Bank on 1st September 1789. By wise management, Wilshere amassed a fortune. He made one very large investment of £80,000 to Whitbread's, the brewing company based in Chiswell Street, London. In return, Wilshere received a large share of the brewery's profits. With this income he purchased valuable estates in Hertfordshire and Bedfordshire, including the Manor of Great Wymondley near Hitchin.

Wilshere's small 'Commonplace Book' (or Notebook) of 1814 reveals that he was aware of national and international affairs, and the need to protect trade and to defend the country. He had commanded the Hitchin Loyal Volunteers during the early years of the war with France, until they were disbanded in 1802. However, in 1803 there was a new threat of invasion by Napoleon's armies. The Volunteers were again 'mustered' and attached to the Hertfordshire Local Militia. Wilshere was their Colonel and The Right Honourable Thomas Brand, the future Lord Dacre, was his deputy.

William Wilshere – "He was a handsome man of middle stature, rather bald and inclined to corpulency, and very courteous in his manners." (F Lucas)

In his career in the legal profession Wilshere became a Justice of the Peace for the County of Hertfordshire in July 1805, and also for Bedfordshire in April 1806. Two years later, in July 1808, he was called to the Bar at Lincoln's Inn, London. These positions gave him broad experience and many responsibilities.

The Wilshere family in Hitchin were members of the Independent Church in Dead Street, where there stood a substantial Meeting House *"built in 1690 with 3 galleries, a commodious vestry and a burial ground adjoining"*. William's father had been a Deacon of this church. During the tenure of Pastor William Williams, 1795 to 1812, there were many families in the congregation who were active in local affairs, including Watson Perks, a surgeon and a distiller of lavender, and William Langford, a brazier and upholsterer. Wilshere also secured the post of Deputy Registrar of the Archdeaconry of Huntingdon, from which he gained experience of the workings of the Church of England in that area.

Through the different facets of his busy life in the law and business, landownership and stewardships, and his church, Wilshere had every opportunity to meet and deal with a diversity of people, the able and the less able, the rich and the poor, the healthy and the sick. There was in late Georgian Britain, as always in human history, a very unequal distribution of wealth and of opportunity. But there was also, as usual, sincere concern amongst some of the educated middle classes for the poverty and ignorance of the lower classes, particularly a sense of pity for the neglected children.

LANCASTER'S IDEAS COME TO THE LOCAL AREA

News of the activities and ideas of Joseph Lancaster, the energetic young teacher with his new school for boys in Southwark, London, would have reached the Quaker and other Nonconformist congregations across the country.

At Christmastime in 1803 John Russell, 6th Duke of Bedford, visited Lancaster's Borough Road School and afterwards wrote *"I was so well pleased that I instantly became a subscriber"*. The Duke remained an active supporter for the rest of his life.

After being rescued from bankruptcy, Lancaster wrote in 1807 *"After visiting Canterbury I went to Woburn Abbey and there spent my birthday, where I had the opportunity of being introduced to the Duke of Manchester whose Christian liberality was very gratifying to me"*. Lancaster gave a lecture in The Market House in Woburn and, in 1809, a Lancasterian School was opened there under the patronage of the 6th Duke, who was concerned that *"the children of the whole county of Bedford should be instructed in the manner Lancaster proposed"*. He was following the example of the Marquess of Bute, who had founded a Lancasterian school in 1801 in Luton.

Another Bedfordshire landowner, brewer and MP, Samuel Whitbread of Southill Park, southeast of Bedford, was also actively interested in the education of the nation's children. On 19th February 1807 he introduced his 'Parochial Schools Bill' in the House of Commons. Whitbread knew of Lancaster's Royal Free School in Borough Road and of the Royal Family's support for his initiatives. In the debate in the House, Whitbread said that *"Lancaster has been the object of much opposition from bigotry and prejudice but I believe him to be on every count deserving of encouragement and protection"*. Whitbread's Bill was not passed – it was too liberal and was thrown out by the House of Lords. This Bill would have laid the foundations of a national system of education, just as a similar suggestion had done for Scotland as early as 1696. In England it was to be 1833 before the Government gave financial support for any aspect of education.

Two further Lancasterian Schools were to follow in Bedfordshire – at Shefford in 1809 thanks to Whitbread, and at Leighton Buzzard in 1813.

Between his first lecture in September 1807, and 1810, Lancaster made 19 'missionary journeys' around Britain, covering nearly 7,000 miles in a carriage or a post-chaise. He was a rousing and effective orator; between 1808 and 1810 he inspired and helped to organise the foundation of 95 Lancasterian Schools.

LANCASTER COMES TO HITCHIN

It was on one of these journeys that Lancaster came to Hitchin and met William Wilshere. And it is William Corston, one of the 1808 trustees of the Royal Lancasterian Society, who left us a record of that meeting. In or about 1840 he wrote *A Brief Sketch of the Life of Joseph Lancaster*. It is far from brief, but contains a most enlightening reproduction of a letter written by Lancaster to an unknown person (although we could sensibly surmise it is to Corston himself). In the letter, written from Barnet on the *"18th of 1st Mo.,1808"* (as a Quaker would write 18th January 1808), Lancaster describes his visit to Hitchin – or 'Hitchen' as he spells it.

The letter implies, we feel, that this was a fund-raising visit. Colonel Wilshere was a rich man and perhaps Lancaster deliberately sought him out. His spelling 'Wiltshire' rather than 'Wilshere' possibly indicates that he did not know him before the visit. He could have been 'tipped off' by Samuel Whitbread, whose country estates were in nearby Bedfordshire. Wilshere managed Whitbread's legal affairs, along with those of many local landowners. We see that Wilshere gave money to Lancaster – but as a loan rather than a gift. This confirms that Wilshere was clearly a shrewd businessman. However, it appears that he also helped Lancaster out by giving him a new suit of clothes.

Nevertheless, Lancaster must have impressed Wilshere, for the latter decided to take further action and to establish a new Lancasterian School for his local boys and girls, particularly for 'the children of the labouring poor' of his own town.

He must have quickly analysed the need for 'a day school' in Hitchin, as an extension of the work of his Independent Church's flourishing Sunday School. The visit by Lancaster was the catalyst which led, within two years, to the opening of the then largest day school in Hitchin, and the first monitorial school in Hertfordshire.

Barnet, 18th of 1st Mo., 1808

My Dear Friend

As I do not wish thy mind to be involved in uneasiness on my account more than I can prevent, I just write to say, I saw Wiltshire at Hitchen, I unbosomed myself largely to him, and had his warmest sympathy; he approved my subscription by loan, and will do all he can to forward it. Finding Whitbread was coming through the town at one o'clock to day I waited for him. When he saw me, he seemed delighted; and so on coming up, said—"What Lancaster! so ho! You have been making a fine blaze in the country." Yes, I said; and if my friends and fellow-laborers in the good cause stick by me now, the country is ours. He said "Yes, it is; but I want to see you." I replied, "And I want to see thee. When will you call—on Saturday?" "No, my time will not admit; but I have to see the Duke of Bedford to morrow, at twelve o'clock, in London." "At what time will you call in Dover Street?" "At thy time." "Well, then at Nine o'clock to morrow morning." So here is the whole history, mystery and world of wonders, as to my staying out of town so long. I have no doubt I was providentially directed to Hitchen, for some wise and as yet hidden purpose. However, the labours of the day, and unfolding my tale of sorrows to Wiltshire, made me not only sorrowful but weary. I sleep here tonight; shall be in town in time to see Whitbread and the Duke, and afterwards come to thee, and shall be truly glad, if my dear Fox has come to London, to eat a bit of goose with him at thy house at dinner time. As to thy rest, I only say, I believe in God the SAVIOUR. I once saw the bridge I was not to pass over. I felt convinced I was to pass over a bridge I did not see, but believe ere long I shall. I think on reading this, thou wilt say "and I should be glad to see it too." "Well, "blessed are the eyes of them that believe, seeing; but more blessed are the eyes of them who believe without seeing." I believe God will deliver me and carry on my work, and anoint my head with oil, and spread my table in the sight of my enemies. So in Christian love I say "farewell for the present;" and only add, my great and good Master has paid all my travelling expences as usual, and given me a good journey; and my new livery* is very good.

I remain,
Thy affectionate friend
Joseph Lancaster

* A suit of clothes given him by Mr Wiltshire on his journey.

Lancaster's letter to a friend, as transcribed by William Corston (the annotation with asterisk is Corston's).

SETTING UP THE SCHOOL

Where was this new school to be? One of the many properties Wilshere owned was adjacent to the Independent Meeting House on the east side of Dead Street (sometimes called Back Street, now known as Queen Street). On the property was a commercial malthouse, with a residential house fronting to Dead Street. The buildings were probably timber-framed structures, the house with lath and plaster walls and a tiled roof, and the malthouse a barn-like building with weatherboarded sides and a thatched roof.

Presumably some alteration, repair or even extension of the malthouse was necessary for the change of use to two schoolrooms. Wilshere's Account Books record two payments in 1811 to Twydell Dear, a local surveyor and builder:

1811 Feb 12th: School : Twydell Dear on account   :   £200
1811 July 23rd: School : Twydell Dear on further account :   £300

Wilshere's Minutes of Property Book also records for 1811 *"The expenditure this year, in respect of real estate, has been building (principally schoolrooms in Hitchin)* = £750-0-0". Such a sum was a considerable outlay of capital but Wilshere doubtless wished to start the school in suitable premises.

The building work is recorded in two contemporary accounts. Firstly, the 1812 Report of the Finance Committee of the Royal Lancasterian Institution states –

"The establishment at Hitchin is for boys and girls. The buildings were erected and the salaries of the master and mistress, and other charges of the school, are defrayed at the sole expense of William Wilshere Esquire. The number of boys is 135. The number of girls is 55."

Then William Dunnage in his History of Hitchin (written in 1815) confirms –

"The Lancasterian School is situate in Dead Street and was erected by William Wilshere Esquire for the purpose of instructing and educating 200 poor

Date-stone from William Wilshere's school of 1810

boys and 100 girls in reading and writing upon the principles laid down by Joseph Lancaster one of the people called Quakers. This building was begun and finished in the year 1810."

The rectangular stone plaque set now in the west brick wall of the 1837 Lancasterian Room is inscribed 'WW 1810' and is all that remains of the first school's premises. In a thesis written in 1960, E R Aitken claims that the refurbished 'School Barn' had *"2 storeys, each with a brick floor, but no heating. The Boys' School occupied the ground floor, giving a single large room for 150 pupils, and the Girls' School was above this, and could accommodate 90 scholars".*

G F Bartle maintains, in an article of 1995, that Lancaster visited Hitchin in 1810 for a second time and that *"he reported well on the British School".* It had made a satisfactory start.

FUNDING THE SCHOOL

It appears that, perhaps rather surprisingly, having set up both schools, Wilshere made no further provision for the Girls' School, other than allowing them the use of the building rent free.

The Boys' School, however, was a different matter. As the income of 1d per week per boy would be inadequate on its own to meet all the expenses of the school, Wilshere endowed the school with a house for the Master, four other cottages in Back Street, two in Biggin Lane, and about six and a half acres of land on Kershaw's Hill, behind the school. These provided an income of about £60 a year, out of which the Master received a salary of £40 per year.

Interestingly, two of Wilshere's estate Rental Books record that for each of the years 1816 and 1822 the schoolmaster, Thomas Dimsey, paid a total of £35 rent to the school's founder – £15 for the school house and school and £20 for land.

This seems to be something of a contradiction, and one that remains unresolved. The reports quoted earlier stated that the salary of the Master and the charges of the school were *"defrayed at the sole expense of William Wilshere".* Yet here, the Master seems to be paying rent to Wilshere for the school and schoolhouse.

Was Wilshere expecting his original 'outlay' to be paid back over a number of years through the rent? Was the income from both the boys' fees and the endowment sufficient to enable the Master to pay such rent comfortably, or did he have the extra worry of having to encourage subscriptions or donations from the gentlefolk of the town to make ends meet? Unfortunately we have no way of knowing. Wilshere's Rental Books are mostly numbers, with very few explanatory notes – those quoted above are all there are referring directly to the Hitchin Schools.

THE FATE OF THE GIRLS' SCHOOL

The BFSS 'Survey of Schools' in 1897 lists both Hitchin Boys' School and Hitchin Girls' School as having received Society grants between 1816 and 1820, but there is no record of how much, although the 1817 annual report of the BFSS records that Hitchin was supplied with *"slates, lessons, badges, marks &c".*

Female School,

FOR THE

Children of the Poor.

The Ladies, and Gentlemen, of this Parish are requested
to attend a General Meeting of the Inhabitants, to be held,
at the GIRLS' SCHOOL ROOM, in DEAD STREET, on
WEDNESDAY next, at Two o'Clock, precisely; to enter into
Arrangements, for re-establishing a SCHOOL, for the Female
Children of the Poor, in this Town, and Vicinity.

Hitchin, September 18th, 1818.

Paternoster, Printer, Hitchin.

The financial situation at the Girls' School seems to have worsened after
1816 and it closed sometime after that. Fortunately the closure did not last
long. In the summer of 1818, Paternoster's, printers in the Market Place,
printed handbills announcing a general meeting to consider re-establishing
a school for girls. The Reverend J W Niblock of the Independent Church
next door took the chair. This initiative was successful and the Girls' School
opened again on 1st January 1819, with 91 scholars. It was financed by
public subscription and managed by a committee of ladies elected annually
by the subscribers.

Maria Topham was appointed to be the Mistress of the new Girls' School,
from Michaelmas 1818. She is recorded as having attended the Borough
Road College the following year, presumably for a period of teacher training.

The Girls' School was now a success, but not without problems. By
August 1819 some parents were complaining that the girls had insufficient
time to do their plait work during the school's 6-day week! Thus time had to
be allowed within the school week for 'work sessions'. Perhaps such clashes
were inevitable when the girls' families relied on the income gained by the
girls themselves to make ends meet.

The school also had difficulty, once again, in balancing its finances. The
Ladies' Committee wrote to Wilshere on August 23rd 1823 explaining that,

as the number of scholars had increased, so had their expenses. Wilshere agreed to help by becoming a subscriber of five guineas per year. He probably made only one donation however – he died the following year.

The Girls' School continued to operate alongside the Boys' School on the site until 1929, when all but the infants moved to a new school site. However, the history of the Girls' School and its schoolmistresses is another story.

THE BOYS' EVENING SCHOOL

In 1812, two years after the opening of the day school, an Evening School was set up for boys who were at work all day. Their fees were much higher than those of the boys able to attend the day school – 4d per week as compared to 1d per week.

The Evening School ran for the winter months in the premises of Mr Dimsey's school. It was funded by subscription and managed independently by a committee of local gentlemen.

A small account book kept by John Ransom and held in Hitchin Museum indicates that, in 1816, a Mr G Maxwell was master and had been sent to Luton for training by a Mr J Reynolds. Maxwell was being paid four shillings per week. The account book also shows payments for the simple but essential equipment of the school:

1816 3 dozen candles at 8/6	£1 5s 6d
Bill of B&FS Soc for slates & lessons	£2 14s 8d
Slate pencils	1s 9d
12 copybooks and 100 pencils from Paternosters	8s 0d
Whistle	6d
Knives and books from Gatward	14s 3d
1817 Kimpton Lamp pullies and cleaning	5s 6d
Lamp and appurtenances	£1 13s 3d
E Perks 2 brass lamps	£1 10s 0d
and 1 gallon of best sperm oil	6s 6d
Knives from Gatward	5s 10d
Neckcloths and stockings from Palmers	5s 4d

The knives, neckcloths and stockings would probably have been given as 'rewards' for good work. This is a clear indication that Lancaster's system of rewards was being operated in the Hitchin British Schools.

The last entry in Ransom's account book is early in 1818. An Evening School for boys was restarted in 1827 so at some point, possibly in 1818, the first Evening School closed.

List of Subscribers to the Boys' Evening School in Dead Street, January 1812.

THE FIRST TRUST IS FORMED

For fourteen years, from 1810 until his death in September 1824, William Wilshere supported the British Schools in Dead Street. It seems that he took this responsibility seriously; it is likely that he knew of many young people in his own town and neighbourhood who had benefited from their education there. This must have been a satisfying achievement for him.

Generations of parents and children in Hitchin have ever since had reason to be thankful for his vision and his philanthropy.

In his will Wilshere left the school and endowed property to his friend Thomas Brand, Lord Dacre. In 1826 Dacre set up a Trust to run the school.

The Right Hon. Thomas Brand, Lord Dacre (1774 – 1851).

The Trust consisted of 20 gentlemen of the town, 10 from the Church of England and 10 Dissenters :

Lord Dacre	*Daniel Times Esq*
Rev Henry Wiles (vicar of Hitchin)	*John Hawkins Esq*
Thomas Wilshere	*Joseph Sharples Esq*
William Wilshere Esq	*Watson Perks, Surgeon*
(nephew of the founder)	*Benjamin Tatham, Woolstapler*
Joseph Eade Esq	*Joshua Ransom, Gentleman*
Joseph Margetts Pierson Esq	*Joseph Lucas the Younger, Gentleman*
Henry Crabb Esq	*Robert Newton, Plumber*
William Lucas, Brewer	*William Langford, Upholsterer*
John Marshall, Brewer	*John Thompson, Draper*
Samuel Smith, Maltster	

The reader may remember that the Church of England had attacked Joseph Lancaster and his ideas. It may appear strange, therefore, that here we have Anglicans and Dissenters jointly managing a British School. However in Hitchin, at least, the various denominations worked in harmony. Much credit for this was due to the influence of Henry Wiles, the vicar of Hitchin. Wilshere's first Master at Hitchin was Thomas Dimsey who was an Anglican, and Parish Clerk.

Indeed, the British and Foreign School Society demanded tolerance in its original 'Principles' –

"All schools which shall be supplied with teachers at the expense of this Institution shall be open to the children of parents of all religious denominations. Reading, writing, arithmetic and needlework shall be taught; the lessons for reading shall consist of extracts from the Holy Scriptures; no catechism or peculiar religious tenets shall be taught in the schools, but every child shall be enjoined to attend regularly at the place of worship to which his parents belong."

The aims and duties of the Hitchin trustees were set out in a Trust Deed, which stated that the property was conveyed to them –

"Upon trust, after defraying the necessary expenses of repairs and insurance, for the maintenance of a Charity School, for the education and instruction of Poor Boys, born or residing within the parish of Hitchin or in any adjoining parish, at the discretion of the Trustees, to read and write and cast accounts, and in such other learning and knowledge, as should be thought useful and proper for boys in their situation of life, without interfering with the religious tenets, in which the parents of such poor children may wish to have them brought up, that is to say, upon the principle of the British and Foreign School Society."

The Trustees were to meet at least once a year to examine the proficiency of the children and any neglect of the master. When the number of trustees had been reduced to seven, the surviving trustees had to make the number up to twenty as required by the Trust Deed, still keeping the balance between the Church of England and the Dissenters.

The Trustees, in fact, met quarterly and a committee of five was appointed at every meeting for the following quarter to superintend the admission of boys into the school and their expulsion in case of misbehaviour. The Trustees were also responsible for raising any extra money that was required for the maintenance of the buildings. As soon as they took charge, they and the Master raised the grand sum of £669 16s 0d from the inhabitants of the town to support the school – £131 6s 0d of which had to be spent on immediate repairs to the buildings.

John Thompson, Secretary to the Trustees. He died on 27 July 1877, aged 79.

Of the original Trustees, John Thompson the draper and clothier of Cock Street, Hitchin, became Secretary (jointly at first with Mr John Hawkins). In his obituary in 1877 he was described as *"the last survivor of the original trustees of the British School"*. He had served for a remarkable fifty-one years and all of the Trustees' Minutes for those years are in his handwriting. Even more remarkable is that his son, Lawson Thompson, succeeded him as Secretary and held the post for forty years – and it was he who compiled the extensive 'Lawson Thompson scrapbooks', now held in Hitchin Museum, which have provided much of the local information for this book.

The Trustees were responsible for the British Schools site and all the buildings on it. But as far as schooling was concerned, they were only responsible for the Boys' School. The Girls' and Infants' Schools would remain under the control of the Ladies' Committee, using buildings belonging to the Trust.

Many years later, in 1903, the Hitchin British Schools became an 'Unprovided School'. From that date the Trustees were responsible only for the buildings; everything else, including teachers' salaries, became the responsibility of Hertfordshire County Council. Separate committees of Managers, the equivalent of today's School Governors, oversaw the running of the Boys' and Girls' Schools.

After the First World War, the school became very crowded. Faced with the difficult task of finding a new site, in 1925 the Trustees, together with the Managers of the two schools, handed over the buildings and the endowment to Hertfordshire County Council. In 1926 the original Hitchin British Schools Trust was dissolved – 100 years after it was founded.

Written by Elizabeth Hunter and Terry Ransome

chapter

4

Thomas Dimsey

MASTER 1810 - 1834

In 1810, when William Wilshere set up the school in his disused malthouse on Dead Street, he put Thomas Dimsey, aged 28, in charge and gave him the use of a house next to the school.

Thomas's grandfather, Barnaby Dimsey, reputedly came to England from Ireland in the early 1700s. Thomas was born in 1782, the seventh child of David Dimsey and Alice Rotherham, who had married in 1771. David is listed in the 1801 census as *'Gardener'* living in Cock Street (now High Street) in the centre of Hitchin.

Thomas Dimsey had no teaching experience and so, for a short while in his first year, he went to the large Lancasterian school in Southwark to train as a master.

When he returned, Mr Dimsey was probably left very much to his own devices to run the Hitchin school. He would have organised it according to Joseph Lancaster's monitorial system of education (see panel, page 35), using the older or more able pupils to teach the younger ones. It must have been quite a difficult job as conditions were very basic.

On 10th January 1811 Thomas Dimsey married Jane Agnes Thomson in the Church of St Mary, Hitchin. They had five children; Alice Agnes b.1812, Thomas b. 1813, William b.1815, Eliza Agnes b.1817 and David John b.1823, but both Alice Agnes and David John appear to have died in infancy.

Entries in the old Parish Records detailing the birth and burial of Alice Agnes in 1812, as well as the baptisms of William, Eliza Agnes and David

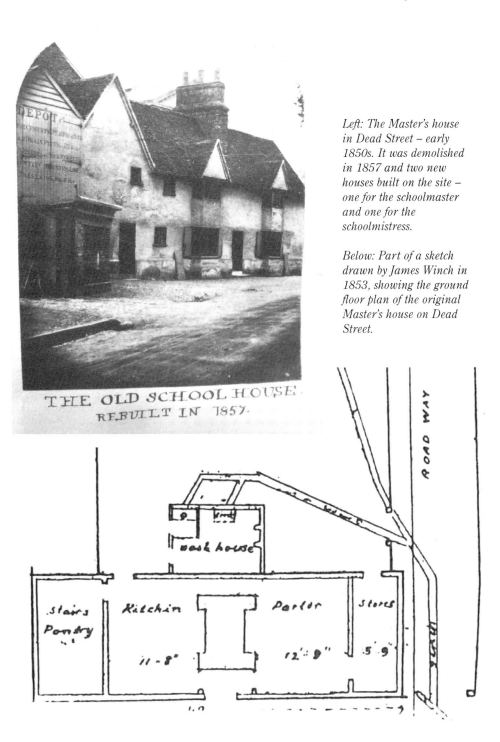

Left: The Master's house
in Dead Street – early
1850s. It was demolished
in 1857 and two new
houses built on the site –
one for the schoolmaster
and one for the
schoolmistress.

Below: Part of a sketch
drawn by James Winch in
1853, showing the ground
floor plan of the original
Master's house on Dead
Street.

Extract from an 1818 map by H S Merrett showing the original malthouse and Master's house.

John, all show their father, Thomas Dimsey, to have the occupation of 'Parish Clerk'. Burial records also show that he was serving as Parish Clerk on his death in 1834. In addition, in March 1828 Thomas Dimsey's name can be found listed amongst the parishioners attending a Vestry Meeting in the Parish Church. All this indicates that Thomas Dimsey was a well-respected figure in the community and was interested and actively involved in all matters affecting Hitchin.

In 1821 Mr Dimsey's wife Jane also became involved with teaching. In March of that year the Ladies' Committee in charge of the Girls' School

LANCASTER'S MONITORIAL SYSTEM OF EDUCATION
"A place for everything and everything in its place"

Devised by Joseph Lancaster out of necessity as a way of reducing costs by using the older children to teach the younger ones, the monitorial system was designed to give a rudimentary education to children whose time at school was limited and whose parents could contribute little to the cost.

The whole system was highly organised with a military style precision. There was an elaborate series of rules and commands – for putting hats on, taking them off, standing up, sitting down and for marching to and from desks. Every seat was numbered and had a slate hanging from it. Above all there was to be order in the schoolroom! A sign saying 'A place for everything and everything in its place' hung over the master's desk in every Lancasterian schoolroom.

The master did little direct teaching himself, his main role being to supervise and test the pupils. He would choose a number of the older or more able children to act as monitors. During school hours the monitors would instruct small groups of 8 to 10 pupils at their desks before taking them to stand at draft stations – semi-circles marked out around the walls of the room. There they would teach them reading, spelling and arithmetic. The pupils would then return to their desks to practise what they had learned. There were numerous schemes of rewards for attentive pupils – merit tickets, badges and prizes. When a scholar had learnt the lesson thoroughly, the master tested him. If he did well, he received a reward.

The monitors themselves received instruction from the master either before or after school. They proudly wore badges to show their status to the other pupils. As well as teaching monitors, there were also monitors responsible for ruling books, mending pens, looking after slates and books and enquiring into absenteeism. All this required a large number of monitors. There was also a monitor-general – or chief monitor – who looked after all the others.

At Hitchin the monitors were usually no older than 12 or 13 years of age and they were paid a small sum for their services.

An extract from the Register of St Mary's Church. Thomas Dimsey and Jane Agnes were married by the Curate, G Parsons. Note the signature of Thomas's elder sister Mary, a witness to the marriage. Another (unidentified) Dimsey has also signed.

recorded that the salary of the Governess, Maria Topham, would be forfeited *"by the impropriety of her conduct which deserves a severe reproof"*. Jane volunteered her services and was appointed as Mistress of the Girls' School, after the Committee failed to get a replacement from the Borough Road School. It seems she continued as Mistress at least until 1831, probably longer. Her appointment is interesting because there is no record of her having had any training and also she was a married woman – at that time female teachers were generally either widows or young single women who usually left if they married.

Maria Topham had found herself pregnant out of wedlock, the father being William Jeeves, a bricklayer from Back Street. Maria quickly married him and, after his death, ended up running the family's building business, then located in a yard next to the school in Dead Street.

In 1824 William Wilshere died. The running of the school passed firstly to Lord Dacre and then, in 1826, was taken over by a board of Trustees, set up by Dacre. They would no doubt have inspected the school and made an assessment of how well – or not – it was doing.

The Trustees' Minute Book makes it clear that they approached their task *"in a serious and businesslike manner"* with the intention of ensuring *"that a good standard of education is maintained in the school"*.

Early in 1827 they 'reappointed' Thomas Dimsey as Master of the school but only *"till next Michaelmas"* (i.e. 29th September), at which time his position was to be reviewed. This would seem to suggest that Mr Dimsey was given a chance to prove himself and improve the school.

The Trustees were concerned about the state the school was in and they approached the BFSS asking them to *"send down a person whom they consider qualified to put the Hitchin School into proper order as soon after the Easter Holidays as possible"*. As a result, John McSwinney was appointed *"Master for organising the School"* from April to June 1827, working alongside Mr Dimsey.

In September 1827 the Trustees confirmed Thomas Dimsey's appointment as Master of the school *"as long as he continues to conduct it to the satisfaction of the Trustees, his salary to be Fifty Pounds per annum and the occupation of the house and garden"*. At the same meeting they determined that an Evening School be set up (or more correctly re-founded since an evening school had run from 1812 until at least 1818), and that the mastership would be offered to Thomas Dimsey at a salary of £10 per annum.

It would appear from the Trustees' minutes that the school was a large one for the size of the town it served. In 1827, the first year full of operation under the Trust, the school admission registers record 189 boys attending during the year. However, in 1828 the numbers of boys regularly attending the school dropped and in October 1828 the Trustees requested Mr Dimsey *"to pay particular attention to the subject and endeavour to insure a more regular attendance, and in all cases to enquire and note down some reason for their non-attendance"*.

It seems that problems at the school continued and early in 1829 the Trustees were of the opinion *"that the present state of the School is much inferior to that in which J McSwinney left it"* and they determined to *"represent the same to the Master and request him to pay more attention thereto, particularly to the training and superintendence of the Monitors"*. They also directed Mr Dimsey to keep a correct and accurate class register which was to be produced to them at their quarterly meetings to enable them to see the progress that each boy made.

The Trustees' Minute Book in January 1831 indicates that Mr Dimsey's son, Thomas Dimsey Junior, was to begin helping his father with the management of the school and in recognition of this he was *"allowed to keep the surplus of the boys' pence for himself beyond £25 per annum"*. Every boy attending the school was expected to pay one penny per week, hence the more boys who came to school regularly, the more income was generated. In his thesis, Aitken calculates that if the school year was 48 weeks long, 150 boys (being the school capacity) attending every week and each paying one penny per week would generate £30 income per annum. If the school was full, therefore, Dimsey Junior could earn a salary of £5 a year from *"the boys' pence"*.

The balance sheet of 1832 (taken from the Charity Commissioner's Report – 1833) shows that the Master's salary was £50 and that the chief monitor (or assistant to the master), Thomas Junior, was indeed paid £5. However, records for July of that year indicate that the Trustees had to make his payment up to £5 because *"the boys' pence having only produced him £2 13s 0d for the last year".* This implies that an average of 138 boys a week paid to attend the school during the previous twelve months.

From this balance sheet it can also be seen that income for the school was only marginally more than expenditure. Balancing the accounts was always a struggle for the Trustees – there was always so much to be done and so little money available to do it – but usually they managed it. A deficit would have reflected badly on them and sometimes they made up any shortfall themselves.

In 1833 Thomas Dimsey's wife Jane Agnes died, aged 40, and was buried on 4th September in St Mary's churchyard, Hitchin.

On 20th January 1834 the Trustees decided that *"from the 30th March Thomas Dimsey cease to be Master of the School and that he be then appointed Writing Master at a salary of £20 per annum".* He was *"required to devote 2 hours a day, 3 days in the week for the purpose of teaching writing on paper".* They agreed to give him a cottage, rent free, in Biggin Lane.

It is quite possible that nearly 24 years of running the Boys' School almost

INCOME	£	s	d
From property endowment	62	10	0
Dividends from £600 3½% consols	21	0	0
Weekly pence from children	27	10	0
	£111	0	0

EXPENDITURE	£	s	d
Master's salary	50	0	0
Assistant to the Master	5	0	0
Paid to Monitors	8	13	9
Books, slates, stationery, rewards	17	3	0
Repairs	11	8	9
Insurance	2	6	6
Quit-rent		1	10
Ground-rents		10	0
Firing for the school-room	1	8	5
Hire of clock for the schoolroom		10	6
Paid an instalment of the loan of £100 borrowed by the Trustees for completing the repairs, leaving £50 now due	10	0	0
Interest on the above debt for the preceding year	3	0	0
	£110	2	9

single-handedly, in what were for the most part very harsh and difficult conditions, had taken its toll on Mr Dimsey and the death of his wife some few months earlier could not have made things any easier for him.

Thomas Dimsey died soon after and was buried on 3rd October 1834 in St Mary's churchyard next to his wife. He was 52. Sadly, no trace now remains of their graves.

Researched and written by Rosemary Ransome

A TIMELINE FOR THOMAS DIMSEY – 1810 TO 1834

Monarchs – George III, George IV and William IV
Prime Ministers – Spencer Perceval, Earl of Liverpool, George Canning,
Viscount Goderich, Duke of Wellington, Earl Grey

NATIONAL EVENTS

1811 – Robert Raikes, founder of the Sunday School movement, dies; Jane Austen publishes *Sense & Sensibility*; The Elgin Marbles brought to Britain
1812 – Charles Dickens born; Prime Minister Spencer Perceval assassinated in the House of Commons
1815 – Battle of Waterloo
1819 – Queen Victoria born

1833 – The Roebuck Act – Government sets up the first fund of £20,000 for elementary education

LOCAL EVENTS

1810

1810 – William Wilshere founds the school in Dead Street
1811 – Hitchin's population is 3,809
1813 – Henry Bessemer born at Charlton House, Hitchin
1814 – British & Foreign School Society founded

1823 – The Port Mill pulled down and a modern replacement built; Dispensary opens in Cock Street
1824 – William Wilshere dies
1826 – Lord Dacre forms the first Hitchin British Schools Trust

1830

1831 – Elizabeth Whitehead's body snatched from its grave in St. Mary's churchyard; population of Hitchin is 5,211; cholera breaks out in poorest parts of town

■ POSTSCRIPT 1

Mrs Yvonne Limbrick, the British Schools' Education Manager, can recall a surprise encounter in 1997. As she was locking up the museum one day, a couple came into the school playground asking if they could have a look around the site. They were visiting Hitchin from Australia and looking for an ancestor – a Mr Thomas Dimsey! The gentleman was Lance Dimsey, from Melbourne, with his wife Dorothy. Lance was the great-great-great-grandson of our Thomas Dimsey.

Thomas Dimsey's son William was born in the old Master's house on the school site in 1815. In the 1841 census he is shown as being the policeman in Therfield. In the 1851 census he is shown, aged 36, living in Silver Street, Ashwell (but his name is written as 'Dunsey') with his wife Mary Ann, aged 41 and children as follows – David J (13), William T (11), Eliza J (8) and Ralph J (5). In 1854 William and his family emigrated to Australia.

Lance provided information on the family's fortunes 'down under'. The son of immigrant William Thomas, another William Thomas, became a teacher and in 1894 retired as Headmaster of Golden Point School, Ballarat East, Victoria after over 35 years service.

The son of the second William Thomas was named David and was born in 1866. He too became a teacher, retiring as Headmaster of Urquhart Street School, Ballarat, Victoria, Australia in 1931. A School Inspector's final report on David reads *"….I place on record my appreciation of the thoroughness, earnestness and efficiency of this teacher. He has proved himself outstanding both as instructor and organiser. An excellent Head Teacher"*. Lance is the grandson of David Dimsey.

Although Lance himself is not in the teaching profession, both his daughters are teachers. What a trend Thomas Dimsey set way back in Hitchin in 1810, and how proud he would surely be!

■ POSTSCRIPT 2

As we were putting this book together, Derek Wheeler, the editor of Hitchin Historical Society's journal, passed to us a letter from Australia. It was from Linley Walker, enquiring if anyone knew of her great-great-grandparents William Merritt and Eliza Agnes Dimsey. Linley's letter told us that *"a family story says that Eliza's father, Thomas Dimsey, was the first head teacher at Hitchin Boys School"*.

Of course, not only could we confirm that but we were also able to tell her much more about Thomas Dimsey and his wife. In return, Linley has told us the following story –

"I was prompted to learn more about my maternal grandfather as I knew very little about his ancestry. I guessed that there was something that he wanted, or felt he needed, to hide. The sad truth I discovered is that Eliza Agnes (Thomas Dimsey's daughter), spent more than forty years in Victoria's first mental asylum

– *Yarra Bend Lunatic Asylum. Eliza's husband William Merritt arrived in Australia with his eldest son Thomas in 1853. Eliza and the three youngest children (John had died as an infant) emigrated to Australia in 1855. The following year Eliza was admitted to the Asylum for the first time. Following her fourth admission in 1862 she remained there until her death in 1900. William Merritt returned to England about 1860 where he died in 1876 in Weston, Hertfordshire.*

"I have found it very sad – knowing what attitudes were to mental illness in those days; the treatment patients received in the institutions; and the shame families felt so that this part of my family story was hidden for so long. Now I want Eliza's story to be out in the open. I want to piece together her life and write her story for the descendents who follow – hence my interest in her family in England.

"Eliza Agnes (Dimsey) Merritt was my great-great-grandmother. Her daughter was Eliza Agnes (Merritt) Gardiner – my great-grandmother – who had three sons: Robert Thomas Harland Gardiner b.1861, James Ernest Gardiner b.1863 and William Dimsey Gardiner b.1867.

"James Ernest, my maternal grandfather, was a primary school teacher – teaching for about 20 years and progressing steadily to become the head teacher of a very small rural school in Victoria. There are other teachers amongst the descendants of our branch – all male, including my brother and a nephew."

We were all very excited when we heard Linley's story – but saddened to learn of the undoubted suffering of Eliza Agnes and her husband William.

■ POSTSCRIPT 3

But that was not the last of our exciting discoveries. To see how we could help Linley with tracing the Merritt family, we looked at a website called 'Curious Fox'. There we found an enquiry which read *"I am researching the Merritt family in the Hitchin and Ippollitts region of Hertfordshire. At least two Merritt brothers migrated to Australia in the 1860s."*

Replying to this enquiry we made contact with Hilary Merritt of Canberra, Australia, who emailed us the following -

"William Merritt and Eliza Dimsey are great-great-grandparents of my husband John, through their son Jesse Merritt (1848-1911). William and Eliza followed the gold rushes to Western Australia but William seems to have had a somewhat chequered career. He eventually returned to the UK where I think he died in 1876, leaving Eliza in Victoria to die in Yarra Bend Asylum in 1900."

We were delighted to make contact with yet another of Thomas Dimsey's descendants and thrilled to be able to put them all in touch with each other.

Written by Terry Ransome

John Lord Brookes

MASTER 1834 – 1842

The Trustees of the British Boys' School had to find someone to replace Thomas Dimsey as Master as soon as possible. So on 7th February 1834 the Secretary of the Trustees, John Thompson, wrote to Mr Henry Dunn, Secretary of the BFSS asking if there was anyone at the Borough Road School who would be suitable. The salary offered was £60 per annum, with the possibility of an increase if attendance figures rose, and free tenancy of the master's house, worth some £15 per annum. A transcript of this letter is shown opposite.

The BFSS recommended John Lord Brookes (the spelling of his surname varies – sometimes it is spelt with an 'e' and sometimes without. However, on his death certificate and headstone it appears spelt with the 'e' and so this is the form which has been used here). He had been born in 1806 and was a teacher with a number of years' previous experience. He had been Master of the British School at Bowyer Lane in Camberwell from October 1831 to October 1832. He was able to supply an excellent reference from his former employer, a transcript of which can be seen opposite.

As a result, at their meeting on the 7th March 1834, the Trustees agreed to engage John Lord Brookes to be Master of the school for a period of nine months *"to commence from Ladyday next"*, i.e. from 25th March, at a salary of £80 per annum (but not the tenancy of the Master's house). Presumably this was intended to be a period of probation to allow both sides the opportunity to see how things went.

Hitchin 2 mn 7 1834

Respected Friend

H Dunn

    I am requested by the Trustees of our School to inform the Committee in London that we are in want of a Master & to ask whether there is any one at present at the Borough Road you can confidently recommend to us. We have at last come to the resolution to dismiss our present Master from the situation he has so long filled, and we are very desirous to meet with a good one to supply his place & as it has been with great difficulty we have been able to get his removal we hope you will do all you can to supply us with a competent and clever Master. I am intending to be in Town in the course of a week and I then mean to call at the Borough Road and more fully explain the circumstances we are under but I may inform thee that we expect the number of Boys will be upwards of 200 and the Trustees authorise me to say they will engage a salary of 60£ per annum and the House to live in worth 15£ per annum with a prospect of an increase if the numbers increase.

    I shall also come prepared to pay the subscriptions due from our Society for two years and also the amount of our School account. I shall be glad to hear from thee at once if there is any one likely to assist us as I should like to communicate with my brother Trustees before coming to town and awaiting thy reply

                I am respectfully
                John Thompson

Transcript of the letter from Mr Thompson to the BFSS dated 7th February 1834.

British School, Bowyer Lane
Camberwell
4th Oct 1832

Mr Brooks having applied to the Committee of the above School for testimonials of his conduct while master, they beg to state that Mr Brooks assumed the charge of the School in October 1831 at which time it was in a languishing state and the attendance of children very small, that in a few months the number of children was nearly doubled and the School brought into a flourishing condition as well as a system of strict discipline established, the progress of the children being considered by the Committee creditable to their Teacher.

    Mr Brookes tendered his resignation without assigning any reason, and relinquished the charge of the School on the 29th ultimo.

The above was agreed to at a Meeting of the Committee of the British School, Bowyer Lane, held 4th Oct 1832
John Elliott
Chairman

Transcript of the testimonial for Mr Brookes from Bowyer Lane School dated 4th October 1832.

43

It would appear that things went very well because on 26th December 1834, at the end of his nine-month trial period, John Lord Brookes was appointed Master of the school *"as long as he conducts it to the satisfaction of the Trustees".* He was paid a salary of £70 per annum and given the use and occupation of the house and garden for as long as he was in post.

This seems a big increase on the £50 paid to his predecessor just two years previously, however it appears that the salary of the Master at Hitchin had always been high by comparison with the average. In the 1840s the average salary for a master of a country school was around £30 per annum. Even later, in the 1850s, the Master of a town school could only expect to be paid between £70 and £80 per annum on average.

The Trustees had done their sums though. When they determined to replace Thomas Dimsey, they also resolved to increase the boys' attendance fees to 2d per week.

John Brookes proved to be a good choice. He was an efficient manager and increased the numbers in the school considerably.

We can surmise that Mr Brookes would be operating to a timetable or curriculum similar to one from the BFSS manual of 1831 :

Morning	9 o'clock	Reading at Draft Stations
	9.15	Drafts for geography and grammar commence
	9.30	Master reads a portion of Scripture
	9.45	Writing on paper
	10.20	Paper writing inspected
	10.30	Slates writing
	11	Mental arithmetic and geometry
	11.30	Senior pupils read Scripture and are tested
	12.00	Monitors' behaviour reports. Hat drill and home.
Afternoon	2 o'clock	Spelling at Draft Stations
	3	Dictation for writing on slates
	3.30	Arithmetic at Draft Stations
	4.30	Class 8 reads to Master and are questioned
	5 o'clock	Reports called over. Master reads Scripture. Dismiss.

In October 1834 Mr Brookes reported to the Trustees that *"the attendance of the Boys is very irregular".* As a result, the Trustees decided *"that the number of Boys on the List be limited for the present to 150 and that the Master have the power of dismissing Boys for irregular attendance and other misconduct ...."*

By 1835, however, the numbers of both boys and girls attending the

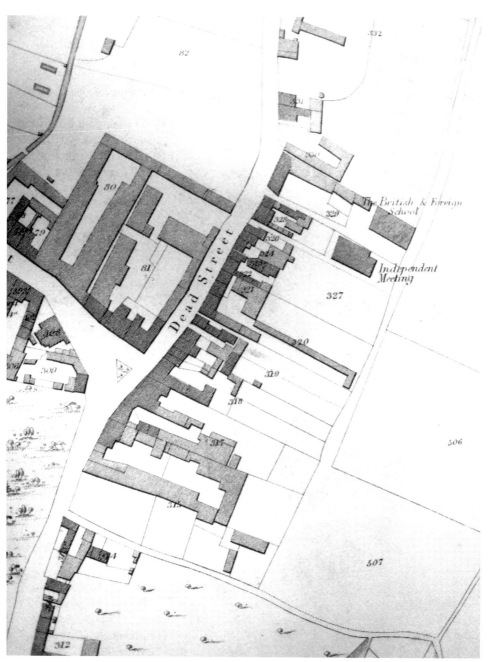

Extract from the 1844 Map of Hitchin by J Bailey Denton, showing the new boys' schoolroom.

schools had increased to such an extent that overcrowding was becoming a real problem – 195 boys and 106 girls were crowded into the original converted malthouse building. There was also a desperate need in the town for suitable premises to set up an Infants' School. The Trustees therefore decided to build a new schoolroom *"capable of holding 300 boys which number they expect from the rapidly increasing population"* so that they could *"establish in their present Schoolroom an Infant School and to enlarge the room now used as a Girls' School so as to hold 150"*.

With the help of a Treasury grant, funding for the new premises was raised. Plans were drawn up by James Jeeves, following Lancaster's own design and measurements, and building work was started by James Raves in March 1837.

The new Hitchin schoolroom (today known as the Lancasterian schoolroom) was almost identical to the one at the BFSS in Borough Road, Southwark – a large rectangular room with wooden pillars beneath high clerestory windows and a sloping brick floor following the original ground level. The total cost for the new room and all the alterations to the existing buildings was £934 8s 9d and by 1838 all the work had been completed.

In July 1838, John Brookes' wife Harriet died at just 30 years of age. The cause of death given on her death certificate was 'Inflammation on the Lungs'. Whatever the precise medical cause of her final illness, it cannot have been helped by living close to the dusty builder's yard next door, or by living with considerable building work on the school site itself.

❏ ❏ ❏ ❏ ❏

In 1842 it is recorded that Mr Brookes complained to the Trustees regarding the rudeness of two of the monitors and they were fined eight shillings each. Presumably this would have come out of the small annual sum they were paid for their services.

Unfortunately, John Brookes died unexpectedly on 27th November 1842 aged 36 years. The cause of death is given on his death certificate as 'Consumption'.

According to local legend, he died in front of his class. However, as the date of death given – 27th November 1842 – was a Sunday, this seems unlikely. Could it be that Mr Brookes was taken ill or collapsed in school and died a day or two later at home? We will never know.

The person shown on the death certificate as present at his death – Mary Banks – was unable to write and so signed her name with an X. We have found Mary in the 1841 census, along with her 16-year-old son, James, living in Dead Street. Mary is listed as being a 'female servant' and James a 'male servant' – both shown residing in the master's house. It seems Mr Brookes had employed Mary as housekeeper, probably after the death of his wife.

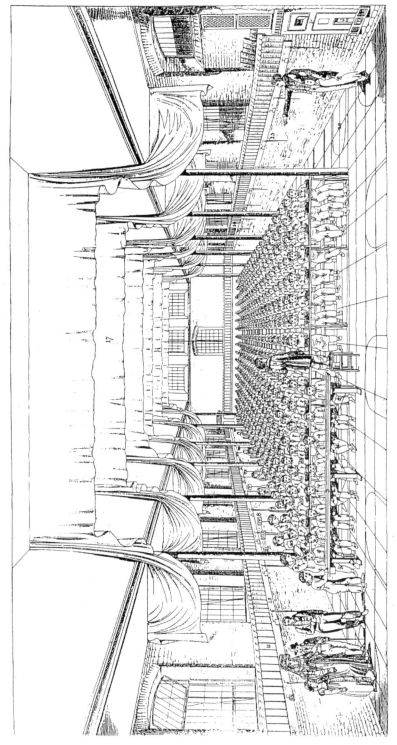

BRITISH SYSTEM of EDUCATION.

INTERIOR of the CENTRAL SCHOOL of the BRITISH & FOREIGN SCHOOL SOCIETY, BOROUGH ROAD.

The new Hitchin schoolroom was almost identical to the one at Borough Road, pictured here in the BFSS Manual of 1831.

47

John Brookes was buried on 2nd December 1842 in St Mary's churchyard, alongside his wife Harriet. Following his death, his relatives presented the Tilehouse Street Baptist Church Sunday School library with 32 books in his memory. We have checked with the church's present-day librarian but, regrettably, no trace of these books can now be found.

Researched and written by
Rosemary Ransome

A sketch of the grave of Harriet and John Lord Brookes in St Mary's churchyard, Hitchin. Wording around the sides reads – "Master of the Boys British School for 8 years".

A TIMELINE FOR JOHN LORD BROOKES – 1834 TO 1842

Monarchs – **William IV, Queen Victoria**   Prime Ministers – **Viscount Melbourne, Sir Robert Peel**

NATIONAL EVENTS

1834 – **The Tolpuddle Martyrs** transported to Australia; the **New Poor Law** provides workhouses for the destitute

1837 – **Registration of births, marriages and deaths** begins in England & Wales

1837 to 1839 – **Charles Dickens** publishes *Oliver Twist* as a monthly serial

1840 – **The Penny Post begins**

LOCAL EVENTS

1834 – Gas lighting comes to Hitchin

1835 – 195 pupils on the British Boys' School books; the Hitchin Mechanics' Institute founded

1836 – New Union Workhouse at Chalk Dell opens

1837 – Lancasterian schoolroom built

1838 – Joseph Lister attends Isaac Brown's Academy, Dead Street, Hitchin (now the Lord Lister Hotel) until 1841

1840 – The (old) Town Hall built

1841 – Population in Hitchin is 6,125

1830

1840

William Ward

MASTER 1842 - 1845

After John Lord Brookes' death, a written request was immediately sent to the secretary of the BFSS asking for a new master. A young man of 20 or 21 by the name of William Ward was sent and took charge until the Christmas holiday. He was then appointed on trial until Lady Day in 1843, when he was confirmed in post at a salary of £70 per annum with house and garden free of rates and taxes.

The 1841 census shows William, aged 19, born in Middlesex, as a School Assistant living in the St. George's district of Westminster with his widowed mother, Martha, and brother Thomas, aged 13.

William Ward himself sheds more light on his background in a letter dated 21st June 1842 to Reverend Dunn at Borough Road. William's father had died around 1829 and William was sent, aged 7, to a British School in Pimlico under the care of Mr William Arnum.

He was a scholar there for five years, rising to be monitor-general after which he was engaged as School Assistant for a further five years. He then found a situation with Mr John Coward (brother-in-law to Mr Arnum) who had an *"establishment for young gentlemen"* in Sloane Street, Chelsea, staying for two years. Ward was also a Sunday School teacher connected to Buckingham Chapel.

In his letter Ward says that he believed his usefulness would be better at a public school working on the British System rather than in a private establishment. He starts his letter rather grandly *"In making application to be received into the noble Establishment of the British and Foreign School Society .....* " He says his most ardent desire *"is to enter the ranks of your Teachers ... on a system which lies so near my heart".*

William Arnum's testimonial to the BFSS asks that the British School deals with him *"as mercifully as you possibly can in respect to finances as his income has been but small and he has to his utmost assisted in the support of his widowed mother".*

Arnum describes Ward as *"mild but decisive in his government and gained the respect and affections of the children. Not in a single instance did I ever detect him trifling with a child....".* The last part of this is an interesting observation. Even then perhaps there was awareness of the need to protect children.

We have not found much evidence as to how Mr Ward ran the British Schools in his term of office, but the Trustees' Minute Book records that he was allowed to employ his brother, Thomas, as general monitor. An entry for 27th May 1844 records that Thomas Ward was given £10 for his services for the year ending March 1844 and that thereafter he was to be paid £2 10s 0d per quarter for as long as the Trustees required his services. It also shows that the Master would be allowed to keep the excess income over £60 from the boys' pence.

Another extract from the minutes for 22nd July 1844 reads: *"The Master be authorised to have an examination of the Boys in the presence of the Parents and others the evening previous to the vacation it being intended by some kindly disposed individuals to give Boys a treat of Tea and Cake."*

In 1845 William Ward no doubt watched in horror as the Girls' and Infants' School was destroyed by fire. The school was insured with the Sun Fire Insurance Office but this insurance only realised £330 towards the £389 cost of rebuilding. More money was needed to re-equip the schoolrooms and, as always, it seems the local townsfolk of Hitchin came to the rescue – raising £259 11s 0d in subscriptions, so ensuring the rebuilding project could go ahead. This is admirable testimony to the good work the school was doing and the support it commanded in the town. The number of pupils attending the British Schools at this time was 565 (260 boys, 90 girls, 150 infants and a further 65 at the Evening School).

Mr Ward, it seems, was extremely fortunate since there is no mention of the fire causing any damage to the Master's house. It is probable that the tiled roof of the house was not as susceptible to sparks as the thatch on the school building.

From 1839, periodic visits to the school were made by Her Majesty's Inspectors of Schools (or HMIs). The Privy Council Committee on Education (the CCE) had introduced HMIs, whose job it was to visit any school given a government grant for building works to make sure the money had been well spent. As the Hitchin school had received a grant for the

THE FIRE AT THE GIRLS' SCHOOL

William Lucas wrote in his diary:

"13th February 1845. This morning between 2 and 3 I was alarmed by a ring at the bell and a cry of fire, about half an hour afterwards seeing that the flames increased I went out and found the most extensive conflagration raging that has ever been remembered in Hitchin. All the range of workshops belonging to Langford & Son, the extensive barns, carriers shops, etc. occupied by W. Hainsworth, the schoolroom, dining room and back buildings at Isaac Brown's school, the stables at the back of the Half Moon Public House and the large building used for the Girls' and Infants' school about 130 yards from the others were blazing at the same time. The firemen exerted themselves to the utmost ..... engines coming from Stevenage, Baldock and Luton and there being a good supply of water, so near the river, by daybreak the fire was very much got under. It was surprising that the whole of Dead Street was not destroyed".

A letter found at Hitchin Museum written by John Thompson, Secretary for the Trustees of the British School, regarding further costs, reads:

"The Girls' and Infants' School Rooms destroyed by the calamitous fire that occurred in the spring of this year have been restored by the Trustees in a substantial manner at a cost considerably exceeding the sum for which the old Thatched buildings were insured — The fittings up of the Schools were not insured — and their cost — hiring and fitting up two rooms for the Schools during the rebuilding, together with some balances due to the Treasurers, and some additions required for the Boys owing to the increase in their numbers will amount altogether to £90."

Thompson also records that subscriptions were promised from:

Lord Dacre	Joseph Sharples
W.Wilshere M.P.	John Bradley Geard
Henry Wiles (Vicar of Hitchin)	William Lucas
William Carling	Ann Lucas
William Exton	William Lucas Jnr.

So far, research has not revealed the source or cause of the fire.

construction of the Lancasterian schoolroom only the year before, it is not surprising that the school would be visited.

HMI Mr Joseph Fletcher paid a visit to the school on 25th March 1845 and reported to the CCE –

"Hitchin – an important institution, based on an old endowment, vested in Trustees of integrity and education, including the vicar, who sought the treasury grant merely to build a new boys' schoolroom which has been done on a very handsome scale with warming and ventilation on a scale worthy to be imitated. The boys' school is sufficiently supported by the endowment and the children's pence and has a good discipline, and a considerable amount of technical instruction, to which the trustees hope to give a higher character, by the employment of an assistant teacher in addition to their headmaster, the numbers being so very great."

The fire in the Girls' School does not appear to have affected the Boys' School.

Quite out of the blue on 21st September 1845, the Trustees' Minute Book records *"a circumstance having occurred rendering it doubtful whether it be desirable to continue the Master in his office. A special meeting of the Trustees be called to decide this question."* However, before they could do that, on 20th October William Ward gave his notice of resignation to the Trustees, asking to leave at Christmas. Unfortunately, therefore, there is no further explanation to be found and we do not know what the 'circumstance' was.

It is not known if his brother stayed on at the school after Mr Ward left. Curiously, we have found no trace of William Ward in any later censuses or other records.

Thereafter the school seems to have been much more fortunate in its choice of Masters.

Researched and written by Jacky Birch

A TIMELINE FOR WILLIAM WARD – 1842 TO 1845

Monarch – **Queen Victoria**   Prime Minister – **Sir Robert Peel**

NATIONAL EVENTS	LOCAL EVENTS
1843 – William Wordsworth made Poet Laureate; Royal College of Surgeons founded	1844 – Tilehouse Street Baptist Church built
1845 – Potato famine in Ireland	1845 – A fire in Dead Street destroys the Girls' and Infants' School building

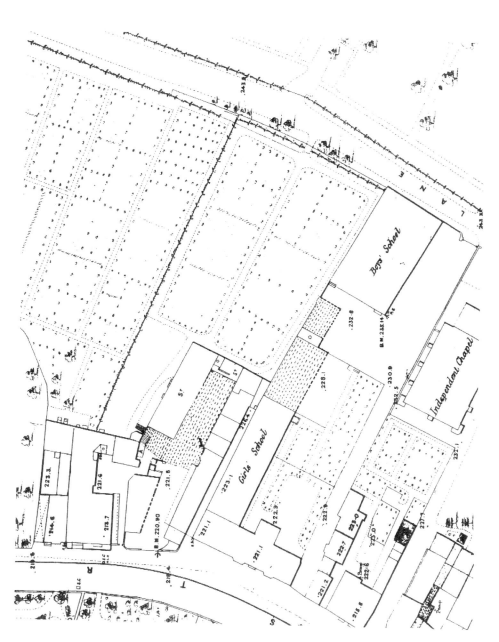

*Extract from the Board of Health 1851 Ordnance Map showing the Girls' and Infants'
School rebuilt after the fire of 1845.*

chapter

7

George Harrap

MASTER 1845 – 1854

After William Ward resigned, the BFSS recommended two applicants for the post of Master to the Boys' British School. They were George Harrap, the Master at Staines School, and William Recket, Master at Baldock School. George Harrap made his application in person and produced satisfactory testimonials to the Committee of Trustees, who appointed him in December 1845 at a salary of £70 per annum with house and garden free from rates and taxes.

The 1851 census shows George (b.1822 in Rotherhithe, Surrey) living in Dead Street with his wife Georgina (b.1816 in Lambeth, Surrey) and three sons, George A (aged 2), Charles E (aged 1) and Arthur (2 months) all born in Hitchin. They also had a 17-year-old house servant, Julia Edwards living with them.

George Harrap's appointment seems to have been a success. Reports show that he was a good teacher instructing his pupils well. He was allowed to employ a chief monitor, approved by the Trustees, at his own expense, which was reimbursed by the Trustees at the end of the year.

In 1846 a new era of education began. With the aim of improving teaching standards and to give schools greater financial help, the CCE introduced the pupil teacher system of education (see Panel opposite). Government funding was made available, but only to schools which were prepared to adopt the new method and submit themselves for annual inspections by HMIs, whose reports would form the basis for continued grant assistance.

THE PUPIL TEACHER
SYSTEM OF EDUCATION

The Pupil Teacher system was devised by Sir James Kay-Shuttleworth to replace the monitorial system. He wanted *"to raise the character and position of the schoolmaster ...to render the school popular among the Poor, as a means of introducing their children to more profitable and honourable employment ....to create in the minds of the Working Class a juster estimate of the value of education for their children".*

By the early 1840s it was felt that real teaching was needed in schools, not just instruction. Children in every school should be divided into groups and the teacher should actually teach each group for a period each day, unlike the monitorial system. To help with this revised form of class organisation pupils, teachers or, even in some cases, assistant teachers were employed.

By replacing monitors with pupil teachers it was hoped to encourage the more able scholars to stay on at school and seek a career as school teachers. Ultimately this would increase the number of qualified teachers available as well as raising the quality of teaching generally.

A number of the brighter pupils in a school would be put forward as candidates to become pupil teachers. The candidates would be examined by an HMI and only those considered suitable would be selected.

The pupil teachers would serve an apprenticeship of 5 years – from the age of 13 to 18. They were to be examined at the end of each year by a School Inspector. If he was satisfied with their progress, they were paid £10 a year in the first year, rising to £20 in their fifth year. Girls, however, were paid only two-thirds of this amount! At the end of the fifth year certificates were issued to those who had passed their apprenticeship. They were then able to take an examination and, if successful, win a Queen's Scholarship which would admit them to a training college for 3 years. Providing they passed the course, they then became 'certificated' teachers.

The Master or Mistress of a school was paid an additional sum for supervising and teaching pupil teachers – £5 a year for one, £9 a year for two and £3 each for others, up to a maximum of £15 a year. The pupil teachers were to receive at least 1½ hours instruction per day, before or after school.

So in August 1847, after 37 years of struggling with very little outside help, and in order to take advantage of the grants being offered, the Boys' School applied to be inspected and was asked to put forward the names of six boys who would be suitable to become pupil teachers. The Trustees' Minute Book records that the following boys were chosen as candidates –

William Olney of Hitchin aged 13½   Reuben Day of Ickleford aged 13½
John Barker of Hitchin aged 15   William Watts of Hitchin aged 13½
William Paul of Hitchin aged 14   Charles Primmett of Ickleford aged 14

On Thursday 14th October 1847, HMI Mr Fletcher performed the first inspection of the school under the new regime. His report on the teaching in the school states –

"The present master has completely re-organised the school which is now in excellent tone and discipline and arranged in large classes of 15 – 25 children under monitors...The writing books are among the best I have ever seen...Instruction in Arithmetic and Reading is excellent in method...."

HMI Mr Fletcher also examined the six pupil teacher candidates and selected all except John Barker (possibly because he was too old). Apprentice Indentures were later drawn up and signed by the pupil teacher, his father and the Trustees. A copy was given to the pupil teacher to keep.

A sectional view showing the new gallery classroom. The Lancasterian floor is levelled and a second gallery installed at the back of the room. From plans drawn by architect James Winch in 1853.

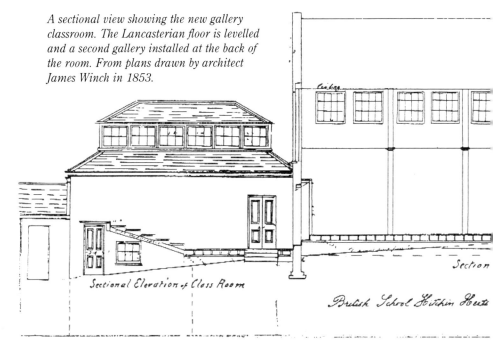

The progress of the pupil teachers was checked annually. Recorded in the Trustees' Minute Book for December 1848 is the following comment from HMI Dr J D Morell –

"All the Pupil Teachers in this school seemed very well trained in the Art of Teaching and likely to hold a creditable position in the Profession should they enter it …..I am to observe however, that more attention seems to have been paid to them as Teachers, than as Scholars – they are by no means so well advanced in their own studies as my Lords would desire – and they all fail in Practical and Commercial Arithmetic in general – This branch of their studies should be more carefully seen to by the Master during the ensuing year."

It would appear that Mr Harrap had some 'teething troubles' setting up and organising the new system!

Although the pupil teacher system was meant to replace the monitorial system, the use of monitors was very popular and the log books show that the Hitchin British Schools continued to use monitors in some roles until very late in the 19th century.

In 1848 George Harrap took the General Autumn Examination of the CCE, conducted by two HMIs, Mr Joseph Fletcher and Dr J D Morell. Mr Harrap passed and was awarded a Certificate of Merit of the Second Division, Second Class and so became a 'certificated' teacher.

The following year, the Trustees' Minute Book shows that HMI Dr Morell made his second visit to the school and reported *"that an additional classroom would increase its* (the school's) *efficiency and if possible steps should be taken to erect one without delay"* but no action was taken by the Trustees at that time.

By 1852 continuing problems with lack of space prompted the Trustees to set up a Committee *"to consider the best mode of building a classroom"*. In 1853 HMI Mr Matthew Arnold inspected the school. Arnold (1822–1888) was the well known poet and cultural critic, the son of Thomas Arnold, famed Headmaster of Rugby School. In his report he said *"The single room in which the boys are taught is a fair one, but a classroom is*

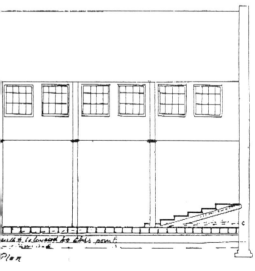

exceedingly wanted". The number of boys on the register for 1853 was 250 with an average attendance of 220.

The Trustees finally decided to build a new classroom for 110 boys, with a gallery – tiered flooring on which the boys would sit. The cost was estimated to be £225 to £250. In addition, various alterations to the large 1837 Lancasterian schoolroom were to be made, including a new wooden floor and alterations to desks, drainage and waterworks. The total estimated cost was £479 10s 5d. A government grant of £200 was obtained and the new classroom was completed by February 1854.

When the Trustees were informed that Mr Harrap had gained his Certificate of Merit in 1848, they applied to the CCE on his behalf for the extra grant of £21 10s 0d due to him on becoming 'certificated' but for whatever reason, it seems that the full amount was never forthcoming.

In 1853 the Trustees increased Mr Harrap's salary from £70 to £80 per annum. However, by 27th January 1854 he had tendered his resignation. On the 1st February the Minute Book records that Mr Harrap was asking to go as soon as possible and the Trustees agreed to *"liberate"* him at the end of the first week in February. William Olney (a former pupil teacher at the school) was quickly put in charge, at a salary of sixteen shillings per week, until a new Master arrived.

⌐ ⌐ ⌐ ⌐ ⌐

But George Harrap went on to a completely new career. The 1861 census shows he moved his family to Waterloo Road, Lambeth and his occupation was now a 'chemist student in medicine'. His sons George and Charles now 12 and 11 – sadly no sign of Arthur on this census – had been joined by John (aged 9, b. Hitchin), Caroline (aged 7, b. Hitchin), Henry (aged 6, b. Stockwell, Surrey), Josiah (aged 4, b. Hampstead) and Ernest (aged 2, b. Hampstead). There are also two servants in the house.

Mr Harrap's wife Georgina, who was six years older than her husband, died in 1874 aged 58, possibly as a result of constant pregnancies and confinements. She had given birth to 8 children over 10 years. Her first child was born when she was 33 and her last at the age of 43.

The 1881 census sees George Harrap aged 59 and a widower, his occupation now being a General Medical Practitioner. He is living in the Vauxhall district of Lambeth with his widowed 70-year-old sister-in-law, Caroline Dodd, and his 10-year-old grandson, George G. Harrap.

George Harrap died in Lambeth in September 1898, aged 76.

George Harrap
Superintendent of the
Hitchin British School.

Researched and written by Jacky Birch

A TIMELINE FOR GEORGE HARRAP – 1845 TO 1854

Monarch – **Queen Victoria** Prime Ministers – **Sir Robert Peel, Earl Russell, Earl of Derby, Earl of Aberdeen**

NATIONAL EVENTS

1845 – Pupil Teacher system introduced
1847 – Chloroform first used as anaesthetic

1850 – New Public Health Act rules all new houses must have a 'water closet, privy or ash pit'
1851 – Great Exhibition at Crystal Palace opens
1852 – Great Ormond Street hospital opens

1854 – Crimean War begins

LOCAL EVENTS

1850 – Hitchin Railway station opens; Local Board of Health established

1851 – Hitchin's population is 7,077

1852 – Walsworth (Hitchin) School built by Mary Exton;
Corn Exchange built at a cost of £2,000
1853 – Galleried classroom built

■ POSTSCRIPT –
WHAT BECAME OF THE PUPIL TEACHERS?

■ WILLIAM WATTS

In October 2007 a Mr Andy Leigh visited the British Schools Museum to look in the admission registers for his great-grandfather, Charles Watts (b. 1837), and to see the very school building to which Charles had been admitted in 1844. Charles had an older brother William (b.1834) and a younger brother George (b.1839).

All three were born in Hitchin and are recorded in the British Boys' School's admission registers, where their father's occupation is given as 'brazier', their religion as 'independent' or 'meeting' and their place of abode as Lyle's (or Lyall's) Row – located just a hundred metres or so from the school gates. The 1841 census has them living there with their father Caleb, mother Lois and a sister Mary Ann.

George died of 'Typhus Fever' in 1850 at just under 11 years of age. He may well have still been attending the British School. By the 1851 census Caleb has died and Lois, William, Charles and Mary Ann are to be found living in Pierson's Yard, still very close to the school.

Of the three brothers, it is William who is of most interest to the British

Schools. He was one of the very first group of pupil teachers selected by George Harrap in 1847.

William Watts is still at the school in 1851, but by 1861 he is a clerk and bookkeeper in London, married to Sarah from Shephall (now subsumed into Stevenage 'new town') and living in St Luke, Finsbury. His sister Mary Ann lives with them.

In 1871 he is a 'bookkeeper to a general merchant'. By 1881, Watts has a new wife Elizabeth and has moved to Edmonton. He is recorded as 'clerk'.

The final record is in 1891. He has moved yet again, to Hornsey, and is shown as a bookkeeper and cashier. Elizabeth is with him, but so too is his mother Lois, from Hitchin, aged 80. William has two interesting guests – for the night of the census if not longer. Two wool merchants from France are recorded as 'visitor'.

So William Watts had learned well. This very timely visit from Mr Leigh and the results of his research pointed us in a new direction. We felt we ought to find out more about young William Watts' contemporaries from 1847.

■ WILLIAM HENRY PAUL

We already had in the museum copies of letters relating to William Paul held by the BFSS archive. They are testimonial letters dated November 1852, provided when he applied for his Queen's Scholarship. They are written by George Harrap, Henry Wiles (vicar of St Mary's church, Hitchin), and John Thompson (Secretary to the British Schools' Trustees). There is a letter from William in very fine handwriting forwarding the testimonials and requesting board and lodging to be provided for his examination at the Borough Road College.

The 1851 census shows William Paul as the second of four children of Thomas and Sarah Paul, both 'staymakers' in Hitchin's Market Place. He is recorded as 'Teacher British School'.

But by 1861 William, at the age of 27, is with his retired parents in Cambridge, working as a 'grainer' (a signwriter or painter). By 1871 he is married with three children and living in Birchington, Kent.

In 1881 there are five children, and the family is living in Lambeth. William employs two men.

The family remain in Lambeth at least until 1901, when William is still listed as a 'grainer & signwriter', as are two of his sons – Albert (31) and Austin (26). Daughter Evelyn (28) is a music teacher.

William Paul did not become a teacher after all, but he obviously found a career that utilised his handwriting skills! He had learned well enough to be able to establish a business and become an employer.

■ **REUBEN DAY**

In the 1851 census Reuben is found living with his family in Ickleford and described as a 'pupil teacher and apprentice'. However, he did not enter the teaching profession. By 1861 he is a 'grocer and farmer of 13 acres', shared with his brother John. By 1871 Reuben has taken sole charge of the farm, is married to Emily and has five children.

By 1891 the family has moved to Leyton, Essex where Reuben is a 'merchant's clerk'. His son William is shown to be a coal agent, his daughter Agnes is an assistant Board School teacher and – saving the best news until last – his other son Ernest is a student at the Borough Road Training College!

By 1901 Reuben has died; his wife is a 'widow living on own means'. Agnes is an elementary school teacher.

■ **CHARLES PRIMMETT**

Charles could only be found in the 1851 census when, at the age of 17, he was listed as 'Pupil teacher and Apprentice'. He was living in Ickleford with his 75-year-old widowed grandmother, who was a 'farmer of 70 acres employing 6 labourers'.

■ **WILLIAM STAPLETON OLNEY**

Knowing we had William Paul's application to the BFSS, we looked in their archives for information on the other pupil teachers. We found one tempting clue – in the lists of Borough Road students for the years 1810-1878, right at the bottom of the page containing the printed list for 1853, is the name 'Olney W S' added in ink. We searched through a box marked 'Testimonials' and there it was – a letter from Olney himself, dated 27th November 1852, to Mr Henry Dunn, Secretary of the BFSS, enclosing testimonial letters from George Harrap, John Thompson, Reverend Henry Wiles and Reverend J F Stuart (curate of St Mary's, Hitchin). Stuart's letter tells us that Olney had served well as a Sunday School teacher at St Mary's for more than two years.

Olney's letter was in reply to the BFSS's invitation to attend the Borough Road College for his Queen's Scholarship examination. In his letter he accepts the Society's invitation to board at the college but declines their offer of accommodation, preferring to lodge with a friend.

We have reported in the main text of this chapter that in 1854, when George Harrap resigned and left, William Olney took charge of the school until the new Master arrived. Could it be, then, that Olney was sent to Hitchin from the Borough Road College after his first year of training to help out at his former school?

The census returns give us more interesting details. William Olney was 16 in 1851 and living in Mill Yard, off Portmill Lane, Hitchin. He is described in the census as 'Teacher in School'. He is the eldest of six children of Benjamin, a tailor, and his wife Sarah.

By 1861 he is married to Elizabeth, born in 1837 in Kimpton, south of Hitchin. They are living in Barton upon Irwell, near Eccles in Lancashire. Here was one of our most rewarding discoveries – William Olney is a 'Schoolmaster National', and his wife is a schoolmistress. By 1881 they had moved to Great Hadham, near Bishops Stortford and William is recorded as a 'Certificated Schoolmaster'. The 1891 census shows the same information. We cannot find William in the 1901 census but he appears again in the Index of Registered Deaths for the first quarter of 1914. It would appear that he died back in his home town of Hitchin, aged 79.

We are very proud of William Stapleton Olney.

Your most obedient Servant
William Stapleton Olney

Written by Terry Ransome
Census Research by Jacky Birch
Additional information: Mr Andy Leigh

chapter 8

William John Fitch

MASTER 1854 – 1899

William John Fitch, c1866

Brian Limbrick discovered much about William Fitch while campaigning to save the schools. His extensive notes, gathered over time, enabled him to share with others his affection and respect for the man who dominated the British Schools for 45 years. They have also provided the framework upon which this record of Mr Fitch's life and work is based.

The boys who attended Hitchin's British Schools at this time, together with the residents of the town, owed a huge debt to their inspirational headmaster.

Strangely though, we might have been celebrating here the life of William John Hodges, for his paternal grandfather was born with that surname. He adopted, however, the maiden name of his

Above:
Sarah Tucker Fitch
(1794–1876).

Right:
Thomas Fitch
(1796–1870).

wife Rachel, a widow of substantial means from Colchester, perhaps in deference to his new father-in-law.

William John's parents Sarah Tucker and Thomas Fitch, a clerk at Somerset House, married in 1820, settled in Southwark and had their first child two years later. There were eight children of the marriage. William John was the third, born in 1826.

While William became the iconic master of the Hitchin Boys' British School, his elder brother Joshua Girling Fitch (b.1824) also had a distinguished career in teaching and education.

William John Fitch had a shaky start in life. He was hampered by a delicate constitution, a club foot and chronic asthma which always plagued him. His poor health restricted him in what he could do. His son, William Joshua, would later recall that for his father *"being prevented from taking part in sporting activities was ever a great sadness"*.

JOSHUA GIRLING FITCH 1824-1903

Joshua Girling and his brother William John
had their early education at a private school
in Southwark. Joshua started work as
assistant master at the Borough Road
elementary school, but continued his
education through classes at
University College. He moved to
Kingsland in Hackney as master of a
school. He took his BA degree in 1850
and an MA two years later.

In 1852 he was appointed by the
BFSS to teach at the Borough Road
Training College. He soon became
Vice Principal and in 1856 Principal. In
that year he married Emma Wilkes.

Seven years later, 1863, he was
appointed a Schools Inspector in York. He
became an education advisor to the
Government. In 1883 he took over as Chief
Inspector for the eastern counties; by 1885 he was
Chief Inspector of training colleges.

In 1896 he was knighted for lifelong service to education.

William followed Joshua into teaching and entered the Borough Road
College in 1846. The Master of the College at that time was the renowned
John Crossley, one of Joseph Lancaster's early star pupils who become a
teacher himself and was Master for 33 years from 1818 to 1851.

William's teaching talents were soon noted and he quickly rose in the
ranks. In a report published in 1847 HMI Mr Fletcher says of him *"A gallery
lesson which I was given by the head assistant teacher, on the solar system,
thoroughly riveted the minds of the children by its familiar, clear, and colloquial
style, with which the boys thoroughly sympathised"*.

After training, William Fitch obtained teaching posts in schools in
Lancashire and Chippenham (at Lord Orrery's Charity School) gaining
valuable experience. But he was destined to spend the larger part of his
career in Hitchin – as Master of the Boys' British School for 45 years.

It was on 27th January 1854 that the Trustees approved George Harrap's departure. At the same meeting they recorded that they had received a letter from a Mr W J Fitch of Chippenham, offering his services as Master. The Trustees invited Mr Fitch for an interview and, being impressed with his references, offered him the post on a six-month trial basis from 3rd April. The remuneration package included a salary of £80 per annum plus the surplus of the boys' pence above £40; free use of the house and gardens; rates and taxes to be paid by the Trustees.

The Trustees chose very well. Not only would William Fitch organise what the BFSS chose to call *"one of the most successful British Schools"* but he also became, according to Frederic Seebohm, banker and historian, *"one of the most valued townsmen"* the parish possessed.

It is surprising, therefore, that despite his success, Mr Fitch was never formally appointed to the mastership of the school after his six-month trial. He is reputed to have continually found this a source of amusement, joking that it was nerve-wracking to be in a job for so long, not knowing whether he was going to be asked to stay.

MR FITCH GETS DOWN TO BUSINESS

An item in the local newspaper, the Hitchin Monthly Record, of January 1855 shows the curriculum that Mr Fitch inherited when he took up his post, and the standards that he was evidently maintaining –

"British Schools. – The annual examination of the Children attending the above named Schools, took place in the British School Room on the morning of Friday 22nd ult" (i.e. December 1854).

"The pupils were examined in the usual system of education, viz: – Scripture History, Geography, Mental arithmetic, English Grammar, History, &c., in all of which subjects they displayed very considerable knowledge. It appears that the system of education pursued by Mr Fitch, Master of the Schools, is productive of the grandest results: the attendance of Parents and Friends was large, and all expressed themselves highly gratified with the system in which the education was carried out."

A cutting from another newspaper (but it is not known which paper) recently found in Hitchin Museum also reports the same examination. This cutting makes it clear that the examination was of the boys from the Boys' School, and that the Girls' and Infants' Schools had been examined the previous day.

Most interestingly, this cutting also reports that the Chair was occupied by the Reverend Henry Wiles and that the English Grammar class was examined by *"a brother of the master, Joshua G Fitch"*.

At the conclusion of the examination William Wilshere Esq. (the nephew of the founder) *"said that he was pleased with the readiness with which the Boys had answered the various questions put to them, and he thought the state of the School did great credit to the Master, and he hoped he would persevere, and not be discouraged if from any cause the number of boys should be lessened".* It is reported *"the number in the school is about 150, but there is accommodation for 250".*

Wilshere's comment here is, we surmise, a reference to the new St Mary's National School being built in Hitchin, just a few hundred metres away from the British Schools, in the area where the permanent market stalls now stand.

It is quite possible that a number of Anglican parents planned to remove their children from Mr Fitch's care to try out the new school, and perhaps they did so.

However, the British Schools had then been established for more than 40 years and had become an institution in Hitchin. The new Gallery had been opened in 1854, but it was time to modernise and a major expansion was agreed. Plans were submitted to the Privy Council Committee on Education (CCE) to replace the original malthouse building, housing the Girls' and Infants' School, that had been substantially repaired following the fire of 1845. The CCE replied in August 1856 to say that –

"The school building should be taken down, at least to the 14 inch brickwork, if not to the ground, and that new school rooms of proper heights and thicknesses of walling should be reared on the old foundation. The playground for the infants should be enlarged by taking in the small garden which adjoins it. It might be as well to take down the old dwelling house and to erect one or two houses for the teachers on the site of that dwelling – this would greatly improve the appearance of the school buildings towards the main street and would be of great advantage to the teachers of the school."

The old Girls' and Infants' School was to be totally demolished and replaced with a new two-storey building. A high wall would be needed to separate the path to the Boys' School, at the top of the site, from the girls' playground below – strict segregation of the sexes was to be maintained.

The Trustees' Minute Book records – 1857 June 17th: *"Plans drawn up, tenders obtained. Sufficient subscriptions were likely to be obtained in addition to the grant from the CCE. Estimated cost £1,914.9.7d. Grant £1,055."* The architect named on the plans was James Winch and the builder was George Jeeves, whose yard occupied the site adjacent to the school.

1858 February 15th: *"School buildings completed and to be occupied this afternoon. Teachers' houses finished in September."*

Mr Fitch had obviously had to move out when the old Master's house was demolished, but there is no record of where he lodged until the new house was ready. In 1859, William Fitch married Sarah Turner and brought her to live in his new home. He was to live there until his death in 1902.

Left and opposite: Plans by architect James Winch for the two proposed new dwellings. The Master's house is on the right, the Mistress's on the left. The builder was George Jeeves.

In 1860 Mr Fitch opened a new adult evening school in what had been the boys' evening school and infants' room, encouraging illiterate parents to *"come and be improved".*

By 1861 there is the first evidence that he was taking an active part in the business affairs of the school. A letter from him to the Trustees, dated 30th August 1861, is recorded in the Minute Book –

"We have in the School none of the very poor, not that they are refused admission or even discouraged to apply, but as other schools have arisen in the neighbourhood I suppose they have found their way to them for reasons I know nothing of.

"Meanwhile the class of boys with which our school is filled is higher and more what is generally termed respectable than I have reason to think it has ever been before.

"Of the 38 Boys who now pay one penny weekly, the parents of
18 are Farmers and considerable Tradesmen
12 Artisans in good employ
4 Small Shopkeepers
1 is Inspector of Police
2 Excisemen and of
but 1 Labourer.

"So I suggest that the weekly payments should be raised; at all events to the extent of making all pay two pence alike."

Mr Fitch also requests permission *"for forming a select class of the upper scholars to receive extra instruction out of School hours and pay extra for it."* The Trustees granted his requests.

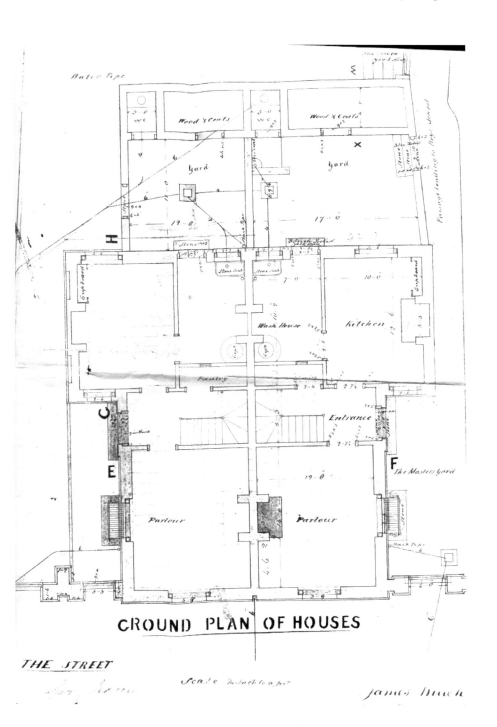

GROUND PLAN OF HOUSES

THE STREET

Scale ¼ inch to a foot

James Bruch

Just two years later, in 1863, fees were increased once again. The notice advising parents of this increase (seen opposite) blames a decrease in the government grant payable. Note also the final exhortation to those parents able to do so, to pay more weekly or to subscribe annually. The school certainly seems to have had its share of boys from well-off families.

We noted that when the Trustees took on Mr Brookes in 1834, they also determined to raise the boys' fees to 2d per week. Now, 29 years later, the fee for those who could afford it had gone up to 3d, while the boys from the poorest families were still only paying 1d.

When in August 1874 the sliding scale of fees was revised yet again, the sons of labourers were still required to pay only 1d each a week, but the fees for sons of the wealthier families were raised considerably, up to 9d per week in some cases. This appears to be the result of another letter from Mr Fitch putting forward the case for a further increase in fees. He also takes the opportunity to ask for a salary increase for himself, suggesting that £200 would be a reasonable figure. On 30th April 1875, however, the Trustees justified the £179 he was being paid as follows – salary £80, from boys' pence £20, 'allowed for' pence £30, for being 'certificated' £20, Evening School £20, pupil teachers £9. A year later, they recorded that, although the Evening School had not been held that year, rather than take the £20 allowance away they incorporated it into Mr Fitch's basic salary.

In 1879 Mr Fitch requested an increase in pay once more. The Trustees agreed to give him a 5% increase – but this meant his pay still fell a good way short of the £200 he was hoping for.

All along, both Mr Fitch and the Trustees realised that some of the poorest families could not afford the school's modest fees and it is unlikely that they ever turned a child away if the parents valued learning, unlike some schools which rejected poverty-stricken, shoeless children. However, while trying to keep the school fees low for the very poor, the Trustees also strived to maximise income from those who could afford to pay.

At times, grants from the Government were uncertain so Mr Fitch organised the collection of subscriptions from friends, 'old boys' and parents.

MR FITCH THE MANAGER

Log books for schools became compulsory in 1861 and are now a great source of much interesting information for local historians. Through the log books we find much evidence that Mr Fitch was a very practical, caring and proactive Master.

The log books for September and October 1863 show that the alteration in school fees was successful –

Sept 7th: *"Reopened school after harvest holidays. ...... during the holidays,*

HITCHIN BRITISH BOYS' SCHOOL.

At a MEETING OF THE TRUSTEES, held APRIL the 18th, 1863, WILLIAM WILSHERE, Esq., in the Chair,—

IT WAS RESOLVED,—

That the Rule respecting the Weekly Payments of the Boys be altered after the Harvest Holidays; and that the Children of Labourers not earning more than an average of Twelve Shillings per week, be admitted to the School at One Penny per week; and that other Classes pay Threepence per week each, except when there is more than one boy from a family, in which case they are to pay Twopence each after the first; leaving open the question of any further charge for the children of those whose circumstances seem to warrant a higher rate of payment.

(Copy)

JOHN THOMPSON,

SECRETARY TO THE TRUSTEES.

THE FOLLOWING STATEMENT IS SUBMITTED TO THE CONSIDERATION OF THE PARENTS OF THE BOYS:—

For many years past, the Income of this School has been considerably augmented by Grants supplied by Government upon the Annual Report of Her Majesty's Inspector of Schools. These grants have enabled the Trustees to carry on the business of the school more effectually than would have been possible had they merely the income arising from the school endowment,—by furnishing ample school materials of every description, and employing an efficient staff of assistants and pupil teachers. The Revised Code, recently adopted by Parliament, which came into force on the first of May last, will have the effect of reducing the amount of the annual grant to a considerable extent; thus it becomes necessary to take steps for meeting this new state of affairs, and the Trustees have therefore had the matter in consideration. They feel that to adopt a plan which would in any way impair the efficiency of the school, is entirely out of the question; but as the majority of the two hundred boys now in attendance are in positions of life superior to that contemplated by the Founder, and as the present rate of payment is unsuitably low,—they find that to raise the school-fee payable by such boys would be one desirable alteration to make. They have, therefore, resolved upon the above rates of payment, to be acted upon when the school re-opens, next September, *after harvest holidays*; and they have no doubt the parents will cheerfully acquiesce therein, and that those who are in a position to do so will be willing to pay a higher sum *weekly*, or to subscribe annually to the funds of the school.

Hitchin, August 19th, 1863.

Notice sent to parents in 1863 by the Trustees advising of an increase in fees.

71

the notices of the alteration in the school fees have been sent round to all the scholars. A few days will shew what effect the change will make......"
October 5th: *"The No. on the books is now again 200. This proves that the increased fees are no injury to the school."*
But there were potential problems with families who lived in outlying areas. Mr Fitch recorded in the log book on Friday 13th November 1863 –
"As many boys live at a considerable distance from the school (50 averaging 3½ miles), we are obliged to allow them to leave early in the afternoon, so that they get home by daylight. I have given notice today that the afternoon school will commence at ½ past one o'clock instead of 2 for the winter months and dismiss at 4. We thus get rid of much inconvenience."

There were always reasons for boys to be absent. Attendance fell sharply at harvest time and if there was any sort of local entertainment to distract the children, such as the annual Baldock Fair, a wild beast show in the Market Place or the 1864 review of riflemen with an exhibition. Full and half-day holidays were given for events such as an agricultural show and ploughing match and the Women's Sunday School treat. On other occasions illness closed the school.

1863 Wednesday August 5th: *"The Review of the Volunteers in the park will be a strong temptation to many boys to play truant, so it is considered better that a half holiday should be given. Experience has shewn that there are many advantages in adopting this plan when the attraction elsewhere is very strong."*

1864 Friday March 4th: *"Very bad weather all the week. In addition to this smallpox, measles and other sickness have for the last few weeks been prevalent. Thus the average this week 152 is very bad for a school of 204 boys."*

1864 Tuesday April 26th: *"A great temptation in Butts Close, Circus at 1d each – keeps away many boys."*

Rewards were used to encourage attendance. In 1872 the log book records that every boy who had attended 400 times or more in the year received a pocket knife. In 1878 Mr Seebohm presented extra prizes to boys who had made perfect attendance – 'never absent, never late'.

Mr Fitch often gave his boys a half day off on November 5, for Gunpowder Day. Other holidays were given for a cricket match, a waxworks show and a missionary lecture.

On at least one occasion he closed the school for his own benefit! 1864 Friday October 14th: *"I have undertaken to give a sort of lecture at Therfield near Royston, and it is better not to hold school as we are short handed."*

There were facility problems to deal with too. On Friday 11th November 1864 Mr Fitch records *"On Tuesday we had a failure both in the warming*

HITCHIN BRITISH BOYS' SCHOOL.

Parents of Scholars are informed that at a Meeting of the Trustees, held on Saturday, the 15th inst., the following alterations were made in the Scale of Weekly Fees payable by the Boys of this School:—

Sons of Labourers and others earning not more than an average of Fourteen Shillings per week, are still admitted by Trustees' Order at One Penny each.

Sons of Artizans and Mechanics, at Fourpence for the first Boy, and Twopence each for his brothers.

Sons of Tradesmen, &c., at Sixpence or Ninepence each, according to circumstances.

This new scale will be adopted at the re-opening of the School after the present Harvest Holidays, viz., on Monday, 7th September next.

The Trustees meet quarterly, and will decide in which of the above grades scholars are to be admitted.

J. H. TUKE, Treasurer.
JOHN THOMPSON, Secretary.

AUGUST 19th, 1874.

In 1874 the Trustees advised parents of a new scale of fees.

apparatus and in the supply of gas, and were very much inconvenienced in both Day and Night Schools."

Other diversions were provided by prominent local visitors such as Lady Dacre, William Wilshere, Joseph Sharples, James Hack Tuke, Francis Lucas, Frederick Seebohm and Canon Harrison.

Sometimes learned guests delivered lectures. In 1867 Harrison came with a microscope and 'A man named Gracey' gave a talk to the girls on astronomy; some of the boys attended. In 1868 the Secretary of the British and Foreign Bible Society had a 'thin time' on his visit because live snakes were being exhibited in the Market Place at the same hour. Other talks noted were on alcohol and the geography of the Bahamas.

Occasionally enraged parents would appear. In 1884 Mrs Spicer, the widowed mother of W R Spicer, called to tell Mr Fitch that her son should not be overworked. She was rather alarmed by his behaviour at night, saying that a neighbour's boy had recently died of 'sums on the brain'.

In November 1887 Mr Fitch admitted a nine-year-old boy from the Infants' School with little hope he could educate him much. *"His sight is defective and he is subject to fits. Does not know his alphabet nor can he count. Copies figures and calls them all K,"* he wrote.

There is a curious record for July 25th 1867: *"Torrents of rain all day. WJF in doors with diphtheria"* – an unlikely self-diagnosis of a very serious illness, certainly at the time.

TIMETABLES

The conduct of the Boys' School is also recorded in the log books, timetables having been pasted or copied into the pages. A detailed 'Time Table & Order of Proceeding, Adopted on the 18th June 1864' and written into the log book shows how reading and writing – and variations such as transcribing, dictation and grammar – dominated the boys' day. 'Cipher' was a daily subject for all standards but the boys were not studying codes and code breaking – 'ciphering' was the third 'R', meaning arithmetic or numbering.

These subjects were practised almost remorselessly, for good reason. The 'Revised Code' of 1862 subjected schools, teachers and now pupils to even more rigorous inspection by the HMIs. Each child was tested in the 3 'Rs', the attendance record was checked, the buildings looked over, and the log book read. Inspection days would have been dreaded. The Government paid a maximum grant of 12 shillings for each child – 4 shillings for regular attendance and 2s 8d for each of the three subjects passed. This was 'Payment by Results'. If the children did not perform well, the school's grant and the teacher's salary would be reduced.

By 1895 arithmetic had taken a more equal place alongside reading and writing, and scripture, geography, singing and 'object lessons' had become more regular and were studied on two or more days each week.

MR FITCH THE MASTER

Mr Fitch tried hard to get parents on his side. He wrote them letters urging them to encourage their sons with the important work of their education. *"This work is one for which you are responsible and which the school is intended to assist you in carrying on,"* he explained in one dated 1st September 1871. *"But the best of us cannot do it half well enough though it amply repays every effort we make,*

Time Table &c.

Standards I. & II.

Time	Monday	Tuesday	Wednesday	Thursday	Friday
9.10-9.50	Scripture / Reading	Reading / Reading	Drawing / Reading	Copy Books / Writing	Grammar / Scripture
10-10.55	Writing / Writing	Transcription / Transcription	Writing / Writing	Drawing / Drawing	Transcription / Drawing
11.10-12	Arithmetic / Arithmetic	Arithmetic / Arithmetic	Arithmetic / Arithmetic	Arithmetic / Arithmetic	Arithmetic / Arithmetic
1.45-2.30	Dictation / Writing	Copy Books / Reading	Geography / Mental Arithmetic	Grammar / Arithmetic	Dictation / Copy Books
2.30-3.25	Reading / Reading	Geography / Drawing	Grammar / Recitation	Spelling / Reading	Drawing / Object Lesson
3.35-4.20	Arithmetic / Geography	Arithmetic / Arithmetic	Repetition / Spelling	Arithmetic / Geography	Singing / Singing

Classroom lesson — Mr Baker

This re-arrangement of Std. I. II. work consequent on the increased staff allows the f.h under Mr Baker to divide the classes —

October 1895 ....

Mr Fitch's 1895 timetable, pasted into the Boys' School log book

In December 1877 Mr Fitch was asked to write a reference for one his former boys, George Cooper, who "attended with great regularity for two years".

He went on: "It gives me great pleasure to be able to say that during the time he was with us here I had every reason to be well satisfied with him. He is a painstaking, attentive lad who can be relied upon to do his best."

George Thomas Cooper (born 1862) had left school earlier to work for Gatwards, General and Furnishing Ironmonger in Hitchin, but in 1877 was now wanting to work on the Great Northern Railway. Mr Fitch's letter is to the stationmaster Mr J L Watkins. George eventually held a post in the superintendent's office at King's Cross. He saw active service in the Great War of 1914–18, rising to the rank of Lieutenant Quartermaster.

He retired from the railways in 1924.

especially when parents and teachers work together. You can make the best of this school for your children by seeing that they are never absent and always in good time." Mr Fitch was no doubt tackling the major changes to the education system introduced by the recent 1870 Education Act, which made elementary education available for every child. In the letter, he refers to *"The new arrangements which Parliament has made in Elementary Schools all over the country are intended to increase and improve the school-knowledge which scholars must acquire".* He informed parents that a new assistant school master had been engaged by the Trustees to help with this.

He went on: *"I believe the teachers of this school are simply anxious for the welfare of the scholars; glad to find and encourage earnestness in their school work and ashamed to treat anyone with unkindness. We look to you for all the assistance you can give us, by showing an interest in the boys' home lessons as well as in the matter of punctuality; and we hope that the future usefulness of the school may be greater than it has ever been."* Mr Fitch was doing his best to encourage regular and punctual attendance. One failing of the 1870 Act was that it had not made attendance at school compulsory. That would not become law for another 10 years.

Another letter Mr Fitch sent out in 1888 repeats his commitment to recruiting parents as his allies. He wrote: *"I have a proposal to make to you which I think you will agree to as it is for the benefit of your son. Everybody knows the value of good, expressive Reading; it is one of the chief things you send your son here to learn, but it comes from much practice as well as good teaching and enough practice is not to be had at school."* He went on to explain how little time there was for reading out loud in class – a maximum of two minutes a week per child. *"I describe all this to you so that you may see my reasons for asking you to encourage your son to read aloud at home and thus greatly promote his improvement,"* Mr Fitch went on in the letter.

"If you will undertake that he shall slowly read out to you or some member of your family daily for a quarter of an hour, I will supply him with an interesting periodical paper to read from. Let me know if you agree to this bargain, and I shall be obliged to you."

Joan Cullen, sister of British Schools Museum volunteer Michael Brockett, remembers her father Bernard Brockett reciting the following poem to her:

Old Mr Fitch is a kind old man,
Tries to teach us all he can.
Reading, writing, arithmetic
But he never forgets to give us the stick.
When he does he makes us dance
Out of England into France,
Out of France into Spain,
Over the hills and back again.

Bernard (b 1909) was a pupil at the Schools, although not of course in Mr Fitch's time, and he recalls this rhyme being recited by the children around the time of the Great War. We think it may have been a skipping rhyme, and the references to France and Spain could possibly relate to a large map of the world which was painted on the playground and used for geography lessons.

⬜ ⬜ ⬜ ⬜ ⬜

We are fortunate to have at the British Schools some notes made by Robert Walmsley and based on interviews with some of Mr Fitch's former pupils. These notes indicate that, whilst Mr Fitch was not unduly strict, he *"gave severe punishment to those whom he thought to be wrong-doers"*. One former pupil, Mr Samuel Burrows, who died in 1973, told Mr Walmsley that when another boy's mother complained to Mr Fitch that he (Burrows) had fought with her son, Mr Fitch asked Burrows why. On being told that the other boy had spat upon Burrows, Mr Fitch's response was *"Spat upon! Madam, you will remove this spitting boy from my school."*

We are told that Mr Fitch *"was a terror to vandals and none seems to remember swearing in school or yard and it is unlikely that he let off poor boys who absented themselves to go gleaning or root-grubbing, but he was quietly sympathetic to them and parents respected him"*.

Mr Fitch walked the school with an ebony office ruler and would tap a boy lightly on the head when he was talking directly to him.

He was often occupied with teaching his own class but *"he had a cane and he could leave his own flock to a monitor while he ensured maximum progress among the lesser fry"*.

MR FITCH THE PERSONNEL MANAGER

There were constant problems running and staffing a large school. Pupil teachers and assistant masters had to be found, encouraged and then replaced as they moved on.

There is a series of correspondence with the BFSS (in their archive) on the subject of recruitment, spanning the years 1859 to 1895. The earliest item, from Mr Fitch's time, in 1859 would never pass the test of the equal opportunities laws of 2008 –

"We require for our Hitchin British School, a second master …. A young man about 20 yrs of age – who has finished his apprenticeship and is preparing for his certificate – Salary £50 pr an. Should prefer a Dissenter. Wanted at once."

This is a letter to 'The Secretary' (of the Borough Road College) from C A Bartlett, written from an address in Paternoster Row, London. Charles Bartlett had a prosperous business there. He was a member of the Independent congregation and had arrived in Hitchin in 1857. By 1859 he was apparently involved in some way with the British Schools. Bartlett's letter resulted in a Mr Collins being taken on by December of that year.

In 1871 a Mr Joseph Leaver joined the staff as assistant master. He was to conduct an Evening School as well.

Mr Fitch wrote to the BFSS in May 1877: *"We shall soon be wanting another assistant master. Mr Kimber, for whom we are indebted to you, is still with us but having succeeded at the late examination in obtaining a certificate he will soon be leaving us for a situation in which he can earn more than we can afford to pay him."*

Mr Kimber had been a good teacher and Mr Fitch hoped his replacement would do as well. He is also keen to see his protégé settled and asks if they have a post likely to suit him. James Hack Tuke, treasurer of the Hitchin British School Trust, provides a reference, stating that Kimber had been with the Hitchin school for about four years. He is *"a good teacher … His moral character is impeccable"*.

Mr Kimber's completed 'Application for a School' form is enlightening. James William Kimber was living in Tilehouse Street, Hitchin. In May 1877 he was 24, and had been a pupil teacher before becoming assistant master. He was certificated 2nd Division in 1876. He was a Baptist but 'not a member', and single.

As to special qualifications, Kimber answered 'yes' to singing, and declared he could play the harmonium. In the sciences he quoted Magnetism and Electricity 1st, Physiology 2nd, Inorganic Chemistry 1st, Physical Geography 2nd. He was asking – perhaps not surprisingly for a man with such skills – for *"not less than £100"* salary. In contrast, Mr Fitch's 'Application for a Teacher' sent to the BFSS offers £60 for Mr Kimber's replacement.

In the event, Mr Kimber stayed until September, having written to decline an offer to go to an urban post as he feared his health would suffer from a city atmosphere. He preferred a small town, a country school or the coast, he said. His replacement was a Mr Alf Gregory, an ex pupil teacher from the Edenbridge British School in Kent.

On 2nd January 1878 Lawson Thompson writes to the BFSS *"One of our Pupil Teachers having left us in October and another at the end of November we are much wanting more help. Do you know of any lad who has served part of his time who could transfer to the Hitchin Boys School?"*

A few days later however, on 10th January, Thompson writes, *"We have lately engaged an assistant master in place of one leaving; a transfer Pupil Teacher is therefore all that we require…."*

By 1883 Mr Fitch was once again looking for a new assistant master, offering a £70 annual salary for *"a good worker"* who should be *"able to teach tonic-sol-fa."*

In 1895 he complains *"We are sadly in need of more help … I have advertised in vain for a third assistant master…"* to receive £60 a year, despite having had *"much correspondence in many directions but everything has fallen through."* Shortly afterwards, however, he was *"glad to be able to tell you that we are out of our difficulties as to the staff, having engaged the services of a young man named White … "*

Throughout his years as Master, Mr Fitch relied heavily on pupil teachers to help run his school. There are however many references to monitors, indeed to 'paid monitors'. They had not entirely 'gone away' with the introduction of the Pupil Teacher system in Mr Harrap's time.

In 1872 for example, Mr Fitch records *"Wm Horn is to be tried as paid monitor"* and then *"Wm Horn who acted as monitor since his rejection as pupil teacher by the inspector has succeeded in obtaining an appointment on the Midland Railway."* But we suspect that by the end the monitors' roles were minor.

We know from the Trustees' Minute Book, that by 1877 the scale of payment for pupil teachers was revised. For the 1st year their pay would be £11 (up from £10), rising annually to £25 (up from £20) in the 5th year.

In 1878 pupil teacher training was shortened to 4 years, and the minimum age raised to 14. By 1896 the minimum age was 15.

One of Mr Fitch's protégés was pupil teacher John Hare. We can trace his progress through the log books –

William J Fitch with assistant masters and pupil teachers, c1890.
We believe Peter Care is seated on the right.

1887 June 7th: The staff are recorded as *"W J Fitch, Certificated, First Class; Peter Care, Assistant; Ernest Dean, Assistant; and John Hare, Pupil Teacher – first year".*

(Note Mr Fitch's status as 'Certificated, First Class' – a great accomplishment and one that most teachers would never achieve.)

Three years later John Hare is a fourth year pupil teacher alongside another fourth year pupil teacher, Wm F Dawes, whom we must assume has transferred in from elsewhere.

1891 July 6th: It is quoted that *"John Hare and Wm F Dawes p.t.s have leave of absence this week to attend the Queen's Scholarship Examination at B R Training College, Isleworth".*

It seems they had to wait a long time for their results for it is not until June 27th 1892 that an entry records *"J Hare has obtained a second class in the Queen's Scholarship Examination".*

In 1895 new pupil teachers are mentioned. The staff are recorded as *"W J Fitch, Master, Certificated, First Class; H D Kittow, Assistant; Maurice Deacon, Pupil Teacher; Frank Sharp, Pupil Teacher"* – but a Mr J H White and a Mr Barker were to join them before the year was out.

On the same page are noted the pupil teachers' instruction times:

Monday	– 6.30pm to 8pm
Tuesday	– 8am to 9am
Wednesday	– 8am to 9am & 6.30pm to 8pm
Thursday	– 8am to 9am
Friday	– 8am to 9am
Saturday	– 9.20am to 11am at St Mary's class for drawing and recapitulation

By 1897 Mr White has risen to assistant; the staff are listed as *"W J Fitch, Master, Certificated, First Class; J H White, Assistant; A A Upward, Assistant; Maurice Deacon, Assistant; * Frank Sharp, Pupil Teacher; E D Hailey, Probationer."*

An annotation for Frank Sharp reads "* *With reference to the recent examination of pupil teachers – Frank Sharp 3rd year passed fairly."* The reader should take note of Frank Sharp. He would remain at the Hitchin Boys' School until 1929, having served under three different Masters – Mr Fitch, Mr Pengelly and Mr Corbett. He then moved with Mr Corbett to the new Wilshere-Dacre School as deputy head.

Mr White is worthy of note too. Having succeeded Mr Kittow as assistant master, he would remain in that position for 26½ years until 1921, when he was appointed Headmaster of St Neots Church of England Boys' School.

AN INSPECTOR CALLS

William John Fitch's Master's Certificate is held in the British Schools' Collection. The certificate was an important document for a Master. It not only provided certification of training, but acted as a 'progress report' – *"Her Majesty's Inspector shall,"* it instructs *"at the visits which he will annually make to the School conducted by the possessor of this Certificate, enter at its foot a brief account of the condition of the School during each of the Five succeeding Years. A Schoolmaster of merit is thus enabled to accumulate evidence of his practical success."*

Five years were required – but Mr Fitch's certificate carries the HMI's comments for nearly thirty.

The certificate was issued in December 1856, a few years after Mr Fitch completed his training at Borough Road, and the first inspection 'in post' was by HMI Mr Charles Alderson in May 1858. His comment reads *"Mr Fitch*

Right: The first page of Mr Fitch's Schoolmaster's Certificate. Above: There are two stamps from the CCE on the second page, to record his certificated status – 3rd Division, 2nd Degree in 1863 and 2nd Division, 2nd Degree in 1869.

teaches a class with animation, and appears to succeed in interesting his scholars". Alderson was to make the annual visits for each of the required five years.

The fifth year's inspection, July 2nd 1863 led Alderson to write *"Upon the whole, this school continues in very fair efficiency"*. That was an important inspection for Mr Fitch; for his certificate carries a stamp recognising him as a schoolmaster certificated to the 3rd Division of the 2nd degree *"by order of the Committee of Council on Education"*. Alongside we read *"Mr Fitch is a teacher of long experience possessing a thorough knowledge of his profession"*.

The school log book records, however, a little craftiness on the part of Mr Fitch when an inspection was due. He records on July 6th, just after HMI Mr Alderson's inspection, *"Excursions and cricket matches occur frequently, and the strictness with which regular attendance is usually enforced must be somewhat relaxed, especially when the visit of H.M. Inspector has been paid."*

The next inspection saw a new HMI visit the Hitchin School. In May 1864 J Laurie recorded *"Mr Fitch is a teacher of long experience and possesses a thorough knowledge of his profession"*. There was an argument though! Mr Laurie insisted that the poetry to be read by Standard V was to be read from a poetry book. Mr Fitch argues back (in his record in the log book at least) that *"the Irish books and some others, tho' containing poetry, do not contain enough."*

Alderson returned for the following two years and commented *"The discipline and instruction are satisfactory"* (June 1st 1865) and *"I am sorry to hear that the Master's health has recently suffered. The percentage of failure in the individual examination is 25. The discipline continues orderly"* (June 1st 1866).

Schoolmasters Certificate.

OF THE   **OF THE**

Second Division.   *Third Degree of Merit*

The Committee of the Privy Council on Education

Hereby Certify That *William John Fitch*, Master of a Student in the *Hitchin British School* Training College was examined in the month of *December 1851* before Her Majesty's Inspector of Schools according to the course of study which answers to the *first* year of normal training.

On a subsequent occasion viz in the month of *May* 1853 having been employed for *one* years in the *Hitchin British* School, he was required to teach a class in the presence of Her Majesty's Inspector of Schools who made the following Report upon his skill as shewn by that exercise.

M*r* Fitch teaches a class with animation, and appears to succeed in interesting his scholars.

Charles Alderson   H. M. Inspector.

The Certificate thus far is limited to the proof of attainments and skill by examination. The Committee of Council are aware that there are other qualifications not less necessary to the success of a Teacher in the management of an elementary School.

Their Lordships have therefore provided, as a means of encouragement to deserving Schoolmasters, that Her Majesty's Inspector shall, at the visits which he will annually make to the School conducted by the possessor of this Certificate, enter at its foot a brief account of the condition of the School during each of Five succeeding Years. A Schoolmaster of merit is thus enabled to accumulate evidence of his practical success.

C. B. Adderley
Vice President

First Year's Inspection (since the last recorded date) Hitchin B.S. (Boys)
The higher classes enrich of children considerably stronger than last year; but the instruction of the ... Charles Alderson H. M. Inspector. June 9, 59

Second Year's Inspection Hitchin B.S. (Boys)
The discipline of the school appears to me good and the instruction is, upon the whole, very fair.
Charles Alderson. H. M. Inspector. June 15, 60

Third Year's Inspection Hitchin Boys. May 27, 61
The discipline is creditable, and parts of the instruction are very fair.
J. Alderson H. M. Inspector

Fourth Year's Inspection Hitchin Boys June 23, 62
The discipline is orderly, and the ... a great part of the instruction creditable.
C. Alderson H. M. Inspector

Fifth Year's Inspection Hitchin Boys July 2, 63.

83

Then, in 1867, HMI Mr Matthew Arnold visits Hitchin once again. He writes on Mr Fitch's certificate *"This is a most efficiently conducted school. The rate of failure is lower this year than last."* (May 29th 1867). But a year later (May 12th 1868) there is a note of caution *"The order is excellent and the higher instruction good; the arithmetic in the middle of the school needs care"*.

In 1869 Alderson reports *"The discipline is good and the instruction of the scholars examined is excellent"* and Arnold continues the positive theme in 1870 *"This institution continues to take a very high rank as a British School"*. A second stamp dated 12th July 1869 from the CCE raises Mr Fitch's Certificated status to the 2nd Division of the 2nd Degree.

But then clouds appear, along with a new inspector Mr C J Robinson. Was he harder to please than Arnold and Alderson? Or were Mr Fitch and his staff going through a bad patch?

1872 – *"The state of the school is hardly up to the level of last year. The dictation and arithmetic are weak subjects."* In 1873 – *"There are many good points about the school, but there is no improvement in the spelling and arithmetic."*

However, this was the year in which William John Fitch was raised to the top grade – Certificated First Class. No doubt Mr Fitch, as well as his family and staff, would have been enormously proud of such an achievement.

1874 was a better year – *"The general state of the attainments is higher than last year."* But 1875 saw more criticism: *"The state of the school is generally efficient, but much weakness exists in the dictation and arithmetic, both of which should have more attention."*

The 'ups and downs' continued. In 1877 *"the discipline is satisfactory and much good instruction is given"*.

In 1881 however, it is recorded that the staff were 'weak'. But the entries end in 1882 on a good note – *"The whole progress satisfactory"*.

MR FITCH THE CITIZEN

Mr Fitch may have suffered from poor health and a demanding vocation but he still threw himself into Hitchin's social and voluntary life. His talents were diverse and numerous. For two years, from 1868 until 1870, he edited the *Hertfordshire Express* during the occasional absences of Mr Chance, the proprietor.

At the request of C C Hale Esq of Kings Walden Bury, Mr Fitch became organist and choirmaster at Kings Walden Church in September 1866. His last appearance there was in January 1871. In the 1870s and 80s he occasionally stood in for Mr Carling as organist at St Mary's and conductor of the Hitchin Choral Society. On Mr Carling's death in June 1892, Mr Fitch took over the role of conductor. He was also a member of St Mary's church choir as a bass singer.

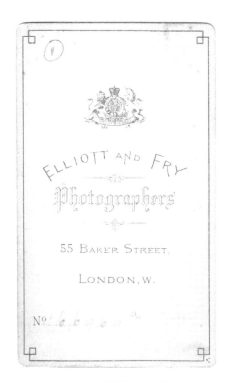

A carte de visite of William J Fitch, c1890.

For six weeks in the summer of 1880 England celebrated the centenary of the Robert Raikes Sunday Schools. In Hitchin, it was Mr Fitch who conducted the United Chapel Choirs in all the main chapels, ending with an enormous joint service in St Mary's Church.

Although he was a devout Anglican, Mr Fitch was happy to let the Quaker Sunday School meet at the British Schools; he even stood in for absent teachers, played hymns for them on the school harmonium and jokingly called himself *"the organist of the Society of Friends".*

Mr Simmonds, a former pupil at the school, recalled when he was 94 years old that Mr Fitch had taught adult men to read on Sunday afternoons at the Quaker School. Mr Fitch's son William Joshua recalled *"In religious matters he was broad minded..... and was very friendly with all the ministers in the town. He occasionally took classes for some of the curates of St Mary's."*

In 1870 Mr Fitch joined the Cecil Lodge of Freemasons who met at Hitchin's Sun Hotel, becoming Secretary and then Worshipful Master in 1875. He was secretary of the town's horticultural society and also enthusiastically supported Hitchin's Mechanics' Institute, founded in 1835 to teach science and *"useful knowledge"* to working men. In fact, members were largely artisans and clerks, and the syllabus grew to include literature, politics and religion.

In 1876 Mr Fitch organised a spelling bee at the Workmen's Hall for scholars and teachers of the Adult Sunday School. He took part in numerous entertainments and read at many 'Penny Readings' in the town and surrounding district; his readings were always a firm favourite. At Offley School (located between Hitchin and Luton) he took part in a charity soirée, offering *"An Entertainment by Sums"*.

In June 1877 he was asked to carve at one of the tables at a vast public dinner in Bancroft, held to celebrate Queen Victoria's 40th Jubilee.

During the 1880s Mr Fitch was the Hertfordshire correspondent for the British and Foreign School Society. When a Hitchin District branch of the Teachers' Association was set up in 1890, no-one can have been very surprised that Mr Fitch gave the first address and was elected president.

In addition to all this voluntary work, Mr Fitch also found time to undertake some studies himself. In 1873, along with the assistant master Mr Kimber, he sat a drawing examination and passed freehand and geometry while Mr Kimber had to make do with just freehand. Under a much-disliked system of 'payment by results' the school would have been given an extra grant for this success.

Mr Fitch found his recreation in books and sea travel, as well as music. He visited Ireland several times and, in August 1883, sailed to Gibraltar and back on the P&O liner *Ganges*. His unquenchable spirit was fired by what he saw and, ever enthusiastic,

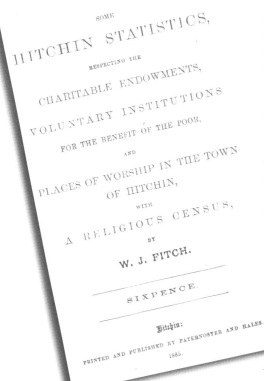

In 1885 Mr Fitch wrote a tract containing statistical details of charitable and voluntary organisations in the town of Hitchin.

QUEEN VICTORIA'S DIAMOND JUBILEE

In 1897 Hitchin celebrated Queen Victoria's Diamond Jubilee. Mugs were presented to youngsters and women and it was Mr Fitch who took charge of the stall and gave mugs to the eager children first. The women were so impatient to get theirs that they rushed forward to grab the rest but were confronted by the tiny figure of Mr Fitch with his arms spread wide, shouting *"Back you women, God has given you handsome enough mugs already and soon you will receive another."*

he brought home two chameleons which he exhibited at the Hitchin Natural History Club. He gave the unfortunate animals to Mr W Ransom to place in his greenhouse but, unlike Mr Fitch, they did not take to Hitchin and quickly died.

MR FITCH AND FAMILY

We can see that Mr Fitch was a caring man who wanted each and every pupil to flourish. He relished all aspects of his busy life and was happy with his work, content in his marriage, proud of his family and rapidly became a mainstay of the town.

Mr Fitch and his wife Sarah had seven children – Ellen Sarah (b.1861), William Joshua (b.1862), Ralph (b.1864), Kate Emily (b.1865), Edith Mary (b.1866), Edith (b.1867) and Margaret (b.1869). Sadly both Ralph and Edith Mary died in infancy.

In 1930 William Joshua said of his father *"Though firm, he was a kind husband and father and it was seldom necessary for him to speak twice when giving orders. His family loved and respected him while his wife spent herself for her husband and children."*

He also remembered his father being *"quite happy when his children were old enough to be gathered round the piano and taught to sing rhymes and children's songs. All the children sang readily and later learnt to read music, joining with their father in the singing of glees and part songs, and became members of the Hitchin Choral Society".*

Mr Fitch was a passionate reader. William Joshua wrote *"My father was fond of Dickens and would sit up most of the night to read Macaulay's 'History of England'. We were encouraged to read Thackeray, Dickens, Lamb, Carlyle, Scott, Pepys and Evelyn, Bunyan and Defoe. 'Tom Brown's Schooldays' was a particular favourite".*

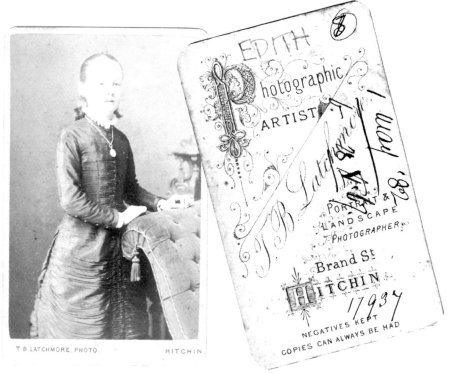

The reverse of this photograph of Edith Fitch indicates a visit to T B Latchmore's studio in Brand Street on 1st May 1882, and that her date of birth was 28th May 1867. It was no doubt taken to celebrate her 15th birthday, but the photographer needed time to get the prints ready for the 'big day' hence it was taken nearly a month early. Is Edith showing off the new locket that would be her birthday gift?

Perhaps it was because it was set at Rugby in the time of the revered Headmaster Thomas Arnold, the father of HMI Mr Matthew Arnold, that Mr Fitch counted that particular book among his favourites.

The census records show that in 1861 Mr Fitch (aged 45) and his wife Sarah (aged 36 and born in Hertford) lived alone at the British Schools in Queen Street, but by 1871 their five surviving children are all listed.

The admission registers show that all four of Mr Fitch's daughters enrolled in the Hitchin Girls' British School, but were quite old when they joined – Ellen was 12 when she joined in 1874, Kate joined in 1875 aged 10 and both Edith (10 yrs) and Margaret (9 yrs) joined in 1878. They are all shown as coming from a private school.

In the 1881 census Ellen is listed as a 'pupil teacher' and William Joshua a 'draughtsman'.

In 1891 son William Joshua is still at home, aged 28, and is listed as a Civil Engineer. Edith, aged 23, seems to be a 'statement assistant', while Margaret, aged 22, has no occupation given. Ellen is recorded in Southwark, living with a schoolmistress and employed as a 'school assistant'. Kate Emily is recorded in Cambridge as a 'certificated assistant', boarding with the headmistress of an elementary school.

By 1901, Sarah has died, Mr Fitch is shown as 'Schoolmaster, retired' and Margaret is living with him as 'Father's housekeeper'. William Joshua is married to Maud and living at 101 Walsworth Road, Hitchin with three children and a servant. Edith is a 'stationer's assistant' in Bishops Stortford, unmarried and living on her own.

MR FITCH'S FINAL YEARS

For all his eminence and the respect in which he was held, Mr Fitch was never a well-off man and he remained in his post until he was 73. The Trustees record on 8th July 1898 that they had had a letter from Mr Fitch saying that he wished to retire at the end of the year. In January 1899, however, he was still in post but unwell.

The log book records on 9th January – *"Serious illness at Christmas has disabled the master + the school has opened today without him"*. The Trustees record his absence at their meeting on 13th January, and that a Mr W Wilkes Smith was being paid to stand in for him.

Happily, Mr Fitch was able to resume work in April. But his last day at work came and, at the close of school on a Friday afternoon in June 1899, the school gathered to mark the occasion.

Mr Lawson Thompson presented him with a marble clock, subscribed to by the boys. A verse, composed by the teachers, was recited by Philip Allen, a senior pupil:

Dear Sir – and honoured through a lapse of years,
  Which to us young ones seems a fulsome age –
To both has come, at length, the closing page
Of our connexion, fraught with hopes and fears.
Some thousands here have sat, into whose ears
  Have poured the cheery notes of counsel wise,
  Instruction good. All worth approved, the prize
That each boy seeks, reward that always cheers.
But we are left to say the word "adieu,"
  And wish you in the golden sunset eve
All blessings rich, and joys not poor, nor few,
  So that the coming years a wreath may weave
To crown a life well spent with honour due;
  Thus with thee now, once more, adieus we leave.

A newspaper cutting reports that Mr Thomson said:
"The boys who are present here this afternoon, and some who have recently left the school, together with the members of your staff of teachers, desire on this occasion of your retirement to give you some small token of their affection and gratitude. During the last forty-five years you have in this room taken leave of many hundreds of boys like themselves whom you educated and sent forth into the world with your best wishes for their welfare; and now at last the time has come when those here present must take leave of you as their head-master. It is an occasion that not one of them will forget."

In the same report we read that Mr Fitch did indeed (as Hine says) admit 3,333 boys to his school. When added to the 160 who were there when he arrived, this means that he dealt with nearly 3,500 pupils during his time at Hitchin.

In recognition of his years of service, the school Trustees gave him a small annuity and allowed him to stay in the Master's house, as his successor Mr Pengelly requested a larger residence.

There is little knowledge of how Mr Fitch spent the last few years of his life in retirement, but we can be sure that he would have taken a keen interest in the comings and goings of the masters and boys who passed his front door every day.

William John Fitch died suddenly in his chair at home on 17th December 1902.

He had made preparations; he had purchased his grave plot at Hitchin Cemetery on 25th August 1883, in perpetuity, at a cost of three guineas. On

William J Fitch stands outside the Master's house in Queen Street – probably around the time of his retirement in 1899. The 'ghost' of a boy can be seen passing between the pillars – he paused perhaps just long enough to register in the camera's long exposure.

11th July 1893, his 59-year-old wife, Sarah, had been buried there. When Mr Fitch's coffin was carried to the Cemetery on 22nd December 1902, it was followed by most of Hitchin, and lowered into the grave to lie with Sarah. The passing hymn *Abide With Me* could be heard in the Market Place; it was an occasion that would never be forgotten by those who went.

Three of their children were later buried in the family grave – Edith (6th October 1911, aged 43), Kate (4th August 1954, aged 89) and Margaret (9th May 1956, aged 87).

Mr Fitch is widely recognised as the finest teacher that Hitchin had known. He had seldom refused to provide a testimonial and his boys held positions of trust around the world.

Sketch of the grave of William John Fitch in St John's Road cemetery, Hitchin.

It is a ringing tribute to this energetic man that a full 26 years after his death, when the Old Boys' Association first met, Alderman Russell declared *"I had the honour of entering the British Schools in 1864 in the days of the great Fitch. There are only 300 of us here tonight, many of the rest are out there running the world; we have telegrams from San Francisco, Moscow, Hong Kong and many more."*

The family were sent numerous letters of condolence after Mr Fitch died. They included the following:

Frederic Seebohm who wrote that Mr Fitch had made himself *"quite one of the most valued of the townsmen"* and that all who came under his influence *"must have felt themselves far better for it"*. He continued *"His real love of English literature and interest in all passing counts made his teaching interesting*

and living in quite an unusual degree".

Alfred Ransom – *"I shall miss him and so will the town for he has been its benefactor for many years."*

Christopher Cross JP, boyhood friend of Mr Fitch – *"I can think of nothing but joy in connection with him. From my heart I have nothing but thankfulness for such a life. He was always a source of brightness and hope to others."*

A TIMELINE FOR WILLIAM J FITCH – 1854 TO 1899

Monarch – Queen Victoria
Prime Ministers – Earl of Aberdeen, Viscount Palmerston, Earl of Derby, Earl Russell,
Benjamin Disraeli, William Gladstone, Marquis of Salisbury, Earl of Rosebery

NATIONAL EVENTS

1855 – David Livingstone discovers the
Victoria Falls; Prince Albert is created Prince
Consort

1860 – Joseph Lister introduces antiseptic
surgery
1866 – Beatrix Potter born
1869 – Suez Canal opens
1870 – Education Act provides compulsory
primary education in England & Wales
1876 – Telephone invented by Alexander
Graham Bell

1897 – Queen Victoria's Diamond Jubilee

LOCAL EVENTS

1855 – St. Mary's School opens
1857 – New Girls' School with Infants' below
and new houses for master and mistress
built; Hitchin Cemetery opens
1860 – Adult evening school begins
1865 – Hitchin Town Football Club established

1875 – Hermitage Road opens

1885 – Hitchin Police Station built in Bancroft
1889 – Back Street is 'officially' renamed
Queen Street; Boys' Grammar School and
Girls' Grammar School open in Bancroft

1891 – Census records 9,510 inhabitants in
the town

The Committee of the North
Hertfordshire Local Board of
the Church Schoolmasters and
Schoolmistresses Benevolent
Institution placed on record its
*"appreciation of the valuable work
done by him"*.

Hertfordshire's Cecil Lodge of
Freemasons – *"Every member was
saddened by the loss that we have
sustained. His most valuable services will
long be remembered and his unfailing*

*courtesy and geniality had endeared him
to every member of the Lodge."*

Alfred Latchmore, Hitchin
Mechanics' Institute – *"He was
known as a devoted supporter of the
Mechanics' Institution in its general
objects and willingly placed his
practical knowledge, wide
acquaintance with popular instructive
literature, and sound judgement at the
services of the committee."*

Kathleen Sarah, Ralph William and Mary Hope Fitch taken by H G Moulden, a well known local photographer, in October 1899.

■ POSTSCRIPT

Of Mr Fitch's children, only William Joshua married. It was to Maud Carling; their children were Mary Hope Fitch (b.1895), Kathleen Sarah (b.1896), and Ralph William (b.1898). William Joshua died in 1940.

Mary Hope was to become a well-respected teacher, who taught for 40 years mainly in Lancashire and then (from 1943 to 1957) in Hitchin.

Kathleen married Stanley Ward in January 1930. They emigrated to Canada where John Carling Ward was born. Kathleen and Stanley later adopted Brenda Margaret, a sister for John.

In Canada, John Carling married Florence Ruth O'Brien and had children David John, Alan Stanley and Caroline Ruth. David John proudly serves his country today as a member of the Royal Canadian Mounted Police.

William Joshua's son Ralph William Fitch had two daughters, Margaret Ann and Joan Mary. These two ladies have both been active supporters and members of the Hitchin British Schools volunteer team since the present Trust was formed in 1990.

Researched by Brian Limbrick and Terry Ransome
Written by Sue Fisher and Terry Ransome

Above: William Joshua Fitch can be seen here with his granddaughter Joan, now Joan Abbiss. Joan's sister Margaret Ann can just be seen on the left. The scene today would be of the large and busy Three Moorhens roundabout on the A602 at the top of Hitchin Hill. The houses behind still stand on the Stevenage Road, overlooking the roundabout.

Left: Margaret Ann Fitch and Joan Mary Abbiss – William Fitch's great-granddaughters, 2008.

Thomas Frederick Pengelly

HEADMASTER 1899 – 1917

When the British Schools' Trustees needed a replacement for Mr Fitch, the applications they received included one from Thomas Pengelly, who had for the previous eight years been Master of the Petersham Russell British School in Richmond, Surrey.

Thomas Pengelly was born in Falmouth, Cornwall in 1852. He lived at Higher Brook Street with his father James, a currier, mother Elizabeth and brother James, born 1858.

Thomas was educated at Falmouth and then at Kimberley Grammar School. He attended the Borough Road College and became a teacher under the London School Board and held several headships, the first being back in his native Cornwall and another at Burdett Hall School. He held certificates in French, Latin and Greek and became a Fellow of The Royal Geographical Society.

At the time of the 1891 census Thomas, aged 39, was living in Salisbury with his wife Elizabeth and son Stanley E. Pengelly, born December 1881 in Hayle, Cornwall. Both Thomas and his wife are described as *"School Teacher, Certified Government"*.

His appointment was confirmed at a Trustees' meeting on the 19th September 1898 but he did not take up the post until 26th June 1899, at an annual salary of £155.

*Thomas
Pengelly.*

Mr Pengelly asked the Trustees to find him a dwelling house larger than the master's house at 42 Queen Street and hence the Trustees were able to let Mr Fitch continue to occupy 'his' house after he retired.

The 1901 census shows the Pengelly family living at 69 Bancroft in Hitchin. Son Stanley, aged 19, is listed as a Mechanical Engineer. (Stanley married in 1904 in Bedford).

Mr Pengelly did seem to be modern in his approach. The Trustees' Minute Book for 1900 records him asking for a typewriter to be provided so he might instruct some of the older boys in this practice.

As Headmaster he was keen for his pupils to experience life outside the school. In January 1901 he took the whole school to Hitchin's Market Square to witness the High Sheriff read out the proclamation of King Edward VII's accession. He often led local outings and frequently let boys off early for Empire Day or to visit the circus, a Wild West show, a football match or a travelling menagerie. In 1903 he took the boys to see the Bedfordshire Regiment march through the town. Sometimes he would even give a half-day holiday when the attendance for the past month had been good.

1902/1903 heralded some significant changes for the school. In 1902 Mr Pengelly joined the newly constituted Hertfordshire County Education

Committee, formed in accordance with the Balfour-Morant Act of 1902. The Committee had been set up in advance of the date in 1903 when, for the first time, all Hertfordshire schools, including the Hitchin British Schools, came under the control of the County Council. Mr Pengelly was teachers' representative on the committee and would serve on it until he retired from the school in 1917.

The Hertfordshire Board of Education suggested renaming the School 'Queen Street Boys' School, Number 106 (undenominated)', but since the British Schools Trustees still owned the buildings it would remain known as 'Hitchin Boys' British School' until 1926.

In 1904, plans were made for two additional classrooms to accommodate 120 boys. Mr Pengelly had written to the school Managers calling their attention to *"the insufficiency of the accommodation for the number of scholars attending the school"*.

Plans were submitted by Walter Jeeves and approved by the Hertfordshire Board of Education in 1905, *"provided the end windows were brought lower down"*. Mr W French's estimate of £479 for the building works was accepted. There were to be open fireplaces *"with No. 3 Manchester grates"*. The path and yard next to the new classrooms were paved with Staffordshire bricks. The sum of £95 was allowed for provision of furniture for the new rooms. Building work was completed later in 1905.

Certificate of Merit awarded to George Cooper (possibly the son of the George Cooper of Mr Fitch's time) for regular attendance at school. Signed by T Pengelly and dated October 1904.

*This 1975 photograph shows the great Lancasterian schoolroom flanked by the
Galleried Classroom (left) and the 1905 Edwardian Classrooms (right). The 1907
Headmaster's study has its windows boarded up. A toilet block can be seen in the left
foreground. The study was demolished in 1977 and the toilets in 1997.*

The two new classrooms were built alongside the Lancasterian
schoolroom on the original boys' playground, so an area on the other side of
Storehouse Lane was paved by Vickers and Field Limited. Mr Pengelly
records in the school log book *"Commenced using new classroom and new dual-
desks. New playground a great boon, gives ample room for drill and exercises"*.

In 1907 there were further modifications made in the Boys' School, to
lavatories and water closets, and a study was built for the Headmaster in
front of the 1905 classrooms. In 1910 an iron fire escape was built onto the
Girls' School.

By 1914 the Lancasterian schoolroom had been divided to form a
separate classroom at the back and a new large rear window installed.

During the Great War three 'certificated' teachers enlisted or were
conscripted into the Services. A staff list for May 1916 records Solomon Hill
on war service from September 1914, Ernest Dennis from November 1915
and Harold Brand from February 1916. The County Council would have
continued to pay the men two-thirds of their salary. The absence of these
men caused major staffing problems for Mr Pengelly who voiced his
concerns to the Managers, saying that any further reduction in male staff
would seriously impair the efficient working of the school.

Even so, the military authorities still demanded more. Teachers Robert McKie and Richard Morse were taken on by Mr Pengelly in 1916 to fill the gaps and are shown in the staff list for the 1st May 1917. But in a letter dated 5th October 1916 – we assume to the conscription office – Mr Pengelly pleads that Morse should not be taken away because it would cause great hardship in the school. The loss of Mr Morse would leave 120 boys in the charge of one *"unfortunate young assistant mistress"* – Edith Millard, an 'uncertificated' teacher who had been recruited in October 1914. His plea was heeded, but one year later, Mr Pengelly's successor, William Corbett has to write an almost identical letter to stave off Morse's conscription yet again.

Mr Pengelly did not lose Mr Morse but he did have to part with Leonard Hart, who went into military service on 31st May 1917.

Happily Mr Corbett was able to record in the school log book for 1919 the return to duty of Mr Hill (now Captain Hill) and Mr Brand in February and Mr Dennis in April. We also know that Mr Hart returned safely from war service and took up his post again, as he and Captain Hill are shown in a 1929 staff photograph.

□ □ □ □ □

Thomas Pengelly retired in 1917, aged 65, after 18 years as Headmaster. At his leaving ceremony held in the playground he was presented with a cheque for £32 1s 7d.

Several days later, Mr Pengelly was honoured with a public presentation at the Gymnasium in Brand Street. There he was presented with a gold watch and a cheque for £23 in recognition of his services on the Hertfordshire County Education Committee. Throughout his 15 years on the committee Mr Pengelly had campaigned vigorously for better treatment for teachers and his efforts helped to double the salaries of elementary teachers in the county. He felt strongly that it was not right or fair that teachers should be remunerated by miserable wages. In Hertfordshire at that time only 27 teachers received salaries of over £200.

In newspaper reports of Thomas Pengelly's retirement, Mr Hugh Seebohm is quoted as saying *"Mr Pengelly might be missed elsewhere, but it was just among those at the British School where he would be most missed. He had been a friend to the boys, of immense assistance to the managers, and had put things forward not from a special point of view, but from what he thought was for the good of the school; he was as much a colleague as a headmaster – looking at everything from every point of view, without any meanness, self-seeking or jealousy (applause). On the local school attendance committee, too, his cooperation and work had been valued."*

The reports also say that Mr Pengelly was an extremely good and popular

Staff – School Year beginning May 1st 1914.

Reg° N°

3933 Pengelly, Thomas Certif Jrd 24. VI · 99

22820 White, John Henry Certif Jrd . 14. X '95
Born 14.I '75

·09/1123 Sharp, Frank Certif Untr? I. VIII · 01
Born 26. XII '79

·04/1408 Hart, Leonard Stokes Certif Untr? I. VIII · 04
Born 7. X · 81

not accepted Superannuated Kemp, Walter James Certif Untr? 8. I · 06
Born 15 I. 71

·10/1154 Dennis, Ernest Edward Certif Jr⁴ { 12. IX · 10
Born 11th I. 84 { war service 15. XI '15

·10/849 Brand, Harold Bates Certif Jr² { 9. I · 11
Born 2. XII '89 { war service 29. II. 16

·11/1952 Hill, Solomon Thos Certif Untr² { 29. IV '12
Born 20 XII ·90 { war service 16. IX '14.

Millard, Edith Emily Uncertif 14. X · 14
Born 4. VII '84

·12/861 McKie, Robert C. Certif Jrn? I. V '16
Born 26 X·89

·12/1883 Morse Richard Certif Untr? 19. VI · '16
Born 10. X. 86

A staff list from the Boys' School log book for 1917.

Headmaster *"attracting as many pupils as it was possible to hold; in fact it was the desire of Hitchin's inhabitants that their children be educated under Mr Pengelly".*

A few months later he returned to the school for a ceremony to unveil his portrait and that of Lawson Thompson, Secretary to the school's Trustees. The portraits were hung in the main hall alongside those of the founder, William Wilshere, and the former head, W J Fitch. As the pictures were unveiled there were great cheers and the boys sang:

> *D'ye ken T P in the frame so neat*
> *D'ye ken T P whom we're all glad to meet*
> *D'ye ken T P whom 'tis hard to beat*
> *And we all wish him good luck now and always*

Headstone on the grave of Elizabeth and Thomas Pengelly in St John's Road cemetery, Hitchin. It reads:

"In affectionate memory of Elizabeth Ellen Pengelly called away February 18th 1911 Aged 59 years
'In thy presence is fullness of joy' Psalm XVI.xi
Also of Thomas Pengelly husband of the above called away December 17th 1923 Aged 71 years"

In his departing speech Mr Pengelly thanked his loyal staff and his managers who had done everything possible for the welfare of the British School. However, with regard to the future, he said that there were large educational problems to overcome. The teachers still had to work in a school building which ought to have been scrapped 50 years ago, and often had to teach sixty pupils in one class. He thought that the boys should be kept at school longer and that, during the last two or three years of their school life, they should go out and learn a trade or profession in workshops or business houses.

To the boys, his message was *"go straight"*. He asked them to look at his portrait and to remember always, when thinking of him, those two words. In a moment of weakness they might need something to help them to be strong. When they went out into the world, he wanted them to think about their old school, and to *"go straight"*.

Mr Pengelly retired to Bournemouth. He died in December 1923, aged 71. His body was brought back for burial in Hitchin cemetery next to his beloved wife, Elizabeth. She had died in February 1911.

His obituary in the *Hertfordshire Express* reads:

"Mr Pengelly was a true friend to all the boys who passed through the School under him and he was a great assistance to the local school managers, who greatly valued his co-operation. He was a man with a large heart; he was without meanness or jealousy, and the happy relations that exist today between teachers of Hertfordshire and the County Educational Committee are in no small measure due to his kindly tact and wise counsel."

Old scholars were asked to meet at the British Schools to proceed from there to the cemetery to pay a last tribute to a Headmaster of whom they had so many benevolent memories.

J. Pengelly Head Master.

Researched and written by Jacky Birch

A TIMELINE FOR THOMAS PENGELLY – 1899 TO 1917

Monarchs – Queen Victoria, Edward VII, George V
Prime Ministers – Marquis of Salisbury, Arthur Balfour, Henry Campbell-Bannerman,
Herbert Asquith, David Lloyd George

NATIONAL EVENTS

1899 – The Boer War starts
1900 – Age limit for boy coal miners rises from
12 to 13; Lady Elizabeth Bowes Lyon born
1901 – Queen Victoria dies at Osborne
House aged 81
1902 – The treadmill abolished in prisons;
the Boer War ends; the Balfour-Morant Act
creates local education committees

1903 – Designs for Letchworth Garden City
begin

1910 – Edward VII dies
1911 – The birch is abolished at Eton
1912 – Titanic disaster
1914 – The Great War (World War I) begins
1917 – The Royal family change their name
from Saxe-Coburg-Gotha to Windsor

LOCAL EVENTS

1901 – Population in Hitchin is 10,788

1902 – William J. Fitch dies in Headmaster's
House

1903 – The British Schools come under
County Council control; the pig and cattle
market in Bancroft closes
1905 – Edwardian classrooms built on side
of Lancasterian schoolroom; boys play a
football match against St. Mary's school,
part of the "Wix" shield contest – named
after HM Inspector E Wix; New post office in
Brand Street built
1906 – New playground in Storehouse Lane
paved by Vickers & Field Ltd
1907 – Supply of coal to Queen Street
Schools for one year costs 19/6d
1908 – Girls' Grammar School moves to
Windmill Hill site

1913 – Hitchin Playhouse built

William Henry Corbett

HEADMASTER 1917 – 1929

William Corbett was born in 1872 in Harrington, Cumberland, the middle son of seven children. His parents were William and Jane; William senior was a general labourer born in the Isle of Man.

Mr Corbett trained at Burleigh National School in Somerset and then at St. John's College, Battersea. The 1901 census finds him, aged 29, living at Chestnut Street, Darlington. He is described as a Board School teacher and is living with Edwin Blair and Benjamin Schofield, also Board School teachers, and Benjamin's widowed mother, Annie, who kept house for them.

Mr Corbett was an assistant master at schools in Ottery St. Mary, Devon; Cowes in the Isle of Wight, and St. Saviour's in Southwark. He also held headships at Baltonsborough, Somerset and West Grinstead, Sussex. He had been Headmaster for six and a half years at East Parade Boys' School, Horsham, Sussex before coming to Hitchin.

On the occasion of Thomas Pengelly's imminent retirement, the school Managers met to consider the 153 applications received for the position of Headmaster. They narrowed these down to ten, then five. The final candidates were W H Corbett from Horsham, J G Dale from Aldbury, Mr Symes from Stevenage, C A Robinson from Knebworth and A H Spikesman from Hertingfordbury (who later became Headmaster at the nearby St Mary's Church of England School).

William Corbett was unanimously elected and took charge of the school

*William
Corbett.*

on the 10th September 1917. He was 45 years old, described as a short, plump gentleman, a keen horticulturist and a livelier man than his predecessor. He viewed the old school buildings as inconvenient and antiquated. His first entry in the school log book shows his first impressions of the school he had taken over. It reads –

"The school is worked too much as a number of separate units. Each teacher does not appear to have acquaintance with the methods adopted either in the class below or above. The lower classes are in a shockingly weak state. There is apparently no groundwork and the teachers are working at a great disadvantage. Reading is especially weak and it will take some considerable time to pull it up. Hence the intelligence is a very low average. Corporate life in the school is lacking and there is no school spirit."

However, when HMI Mr W Whiting visited in 1918 he reported –

"In spite of the difficulties caused by the serious defects of the premises the new headmaster has within a year affected a marked improvement in general discipline and style of work. An excellent monitorial system has been introduced and some really remarkable work has been done in bringing the two acres of school garden into cultivation. The newly introduced habit of staying at school until 15 will need to be taken into account in providing accommodation in future."

As early as 1919 the Trustees' Minute Book records that a new school is required as they deem it impossible to make the old school buildings satisfactory.

Two sites were mentioned: (1) land near the gas works, belonging to Hitchin United Charities and (2) a field belonging to Mr A Ransom (a British Schools' Trustee), in Fishponds Road. The search for a new site would continue for the next 5 years.

Mr Corbett was an enthusiastic gardener and wanted to make real educational use of the school gardens. He himself gave additional classes to boys in the grounds in good weather.

Frequent entries in the log book record his enthusiasm – *"Garden choked with weeds, presenting the appearance of a wilderness"*. *"Supply of forks arrived today (August), ordered in July"*. *"Senior boys went to Oughtonhead to study the environment"*. In September 1919 he wrote *"An excellent show of school garden produce was exhibited. Many parents were present. Over £10 was distributed to the boys in prizes."*

❏ ❏ ❏ ❏ ❏

Just as in the times of the earlier masters, non-attendance continued to be a problem at the school. There were many reasons. Apart from illness and epidemics, others included bad weather, the farming season, market day, visiting fairs and not having boots to wear. In January 1918 Mr Corbett wrote in the log book *"90 boys absent this afternoon mainly in the queue to obtain margarine. Wrote letter to Education sub-committee on the subject."*

But remember, at this time Britain was still fighting the Great War and life would have been difficult.

There were problems of poor wages – *"Today I made out the salary sheet, owing to the extraordinary working of the salary scale the headmaster receives less than his first assistant."*

There were staff shortages – *"Two teachers short. 120 boys without a master, no help forthcoming from Hertford"* – as well as overcrowded classes and inadequate buildings. On top of all this, Mr Corbett also tried to cater for the needs of the higher scholars as well as dealing with *"backward children"* (Corbett's words) by means of a special class taken in a shed in the school garden.

Little wonder then that the log book entry for June 1922 reads – *"Master visits doctor. Doctor advises a month's rest, as his nerves in a bad state and advised to take things steadily or he may have a serious nervous breakdown."*

By 1923 it seems that Mr Corbett had recovered. He re-arranged classes in general work, woodwork and gardening. Classes were divided into teams or 'houses' named after four honoured men connected with the history of the British Schools – DACRE, named after the Trust's founder Lord Dacre; WILSHERE, named after the school's founder William Wilshere; FITCH,

A Queen Street Boys' School Gardening Class, 1922. The gardens were at the back of the school.

named after W J Fitch, the longest serving headmaster; and THOMPSON, named after John Thompson, the school's first Secretary and Trustee.

In Mr Corbett's time, the school colours were royal blue and gold – the colours of the Wilshere family. We do not know when these colours were adopted, but it is unlikely that there was any money at home or in school for such 'niceties' in the 19th century.

On 16th May 1924, having failed to find a suitable site for a new school, the British Schools' Trustees (who were still responsible for the school buildings) along with the Managers of the Boys' School and the Managers of the Girls' School, agreed that all the Trust's assets, including the school buildings and the land on which they stood, along with large tracts of land beyond Storehouse Lane, would be transferred to the County Council.

The Deed of Conveyance is dated 22nd December 1925. From that date the British Schools were completely in County hands and became known as The Queen Street School. The British Schools Trust was finally wound up in 1926, 100 years after it had been founded.

In March 1926 William Corbett was elected president of the Hertfordshire Teachers' Association. That same month he wrote his last letter to British Schools' Trustee, Mr Seebohm. The letter reads:

> *"As this will be practically the last meeting of the Managers of The British Boys School, the staff wishes to express to you and the committee, the most sincere thanks for the confidence and trust you have always bestowed in them.*
>
> *The relationship has always been most happy, and it has always been a pleasure to give loyal and willing service.*
>
> *We trust that the traditions of the British School will long remain and that when the time comes the atmosphere may be transferred to the new buildings.*
>
> *It is with deep regret that we cease to exist as the British School but we accept the inevitable and again tender our sincere thanks for the happy conditions which have been maintained and made our work a real joy under trying circumstances.*
>
> *Very sincerely yours*
>
> *W H Corbett"*

Hertfordshire County Council had determined to move all the Queen Street pupils to a new school they were to build in Fishponds Road, Hitchin. The new school was to be named after both the founder of the British Schools,

Class 4a, c1925. Taken in the Lancasterian Schoolroom with Mr Corbett (on left) and Captain Hill. Portraits of former Headmasters W J Fitch and T Pengelly can be seen on the wall behind them.

The Senior Class in the gallery classroom, 1926. Mr Corbett and Mr Sharp can be seen standing on the right. Note the gas lighting – in use until 1938.

and the founder of the Trust that ran it – Wilshere-Dacre School was to open in 1929. In preparation for the closure of the British Schools Mr Corbett founded The Hitchin British Schools' Old Boys Association. Their first reunion was held in March 1928 and became an annual event until at least 1997.

In the end the move was not to be quite as planned. While there was room for the junior boys and girls in the new school, the infants had to remain at Queen Street – the old school buildings had been given a reprieve!

As the opening of the new Wilshere-Dacre School approached, life at the old British Schools began to wind down.

The entry in the school log book for October 1928 reads – *"The garden plots, except those at the bottom of the gardens, will be disconnected and the time utilised in getting the ground ready for Wilshere Dacre School. Mr Gordon visited school re: furniture. Mr Whittaker, county architect, visited school."*

And for 8th February 1929 *"School closes today to permit removal of furniture to Wilshere Dacre."*

The *Hertfordshire Express* reported the opening of the new school, which took place on Monday 11th February 1929. The scholars had been given the whole day off the previous Friday but most of them lent a willing hand to the

Staff of the Queen Street Boys' School, Hitchin in 1929. From the left – Mr Sharp, Captain Hill, Mr White, Miss Dawson, Mr Hart, Mr Rumbold, Mr Boffin, Mr Kemp, Mr Corbett .

moving operations. One boy, entirely on his own initiative, borrowed his father's horse and trolley and drove it back and forth between the two sites.

Mr Corbett, the last headmaster of the British School, became the first headmaster of Wilshere-Dacre School. Mr Frank Sharp became deputy head, having begun his teaching career as a pupil teacher under William Fitch. Many of the other teachers also transferred to Wilshere-Dacre.

A few years later, on his retirement from Wilshere-Dacre School in August 1932, Mr Corbett was presented with a barometer. He was succeeded by Mr Hector Victor Ferrier, former headmaster of Clay Cross Senior Boys' School in Chesterfield.

William Corbett and his wife retired to Somerset. We do not know when or where Mr Corbett died.

Researched and written by Jacky Birch

A TIMELINE FOR WILLIAM CORBETT – 1917 TO 1929

Monarch – **George V**
Prime Ministers – **David Lloyd George, Andrew Bonnar Law, Stanley Baldwin, James Ramsey MacDonald**

NATIONAL EVENTS

1917

LOCAL EVENTS

1918 – New Education Act fixes school-
leaving age to 14; Women over 30 get the
right to vote; the Great War ends
1919 – Lady Astor becomes first woman MP

1922 – Howard Carter discovers tomb of
Tutankhamun
1923 – Duke of York marries Elizabeth
Bowes-Lyon
1924 – Mallory and Irvine are lost on Mount
Everest
1925 – John Logie Baird invents a working
television system; Agatha Christie
disappears

1921 – The population of Hitchin is 12,829;
Windmill Hill given to the town by the
Seebohm family

1925 – British Schools buildings transferred
to Hertfordshire County Council by Trustees;
St. Mary's vicarage in Churchyard sold and
a new one built in Grays Lane; Demolition of
Queen Street slums started
1929 – Wilshere Dacre-School opens, all
except Infants transfer there from Queen
Street

■ POSTSCRIPT

A mystery photograph (right) is in the possession of the British Schools Museum. It shows Mr Corbett with many of his boys in fancy dress and uniforms in Hitchin's Market Place. The placard held high by the leading boy reads:

BOYS BRITISH SCHOOL
OUR MOTTO
PLAY THE GAME

In the photograph the panel seen just above Mr Corbett's head declares the left-hand building to be 'London Joint City & Midland Bank Limited' – now rather blandly re-named 'HSBC' but still in the same premises. Briggs and Company's shoe shop together with the 'Maypole' grocery is today a hair and beauty salon.

The original photograph was brought into the museum by Mrs Wendy Cant in 2005. The occasion, or purpose, of the photo is unknown. However, a newspaper cutting in the Lawson Thompson Scrapbook in Hitchin Museum tells us the origin of the motto. The report tells us that at Mr Pengelly's retirement celebrations –

"The proceedings ended with Kipling's Recessional, 'the school chorus' and the National Anthem. The chorus written by Mr Corbett was as follows:

> *We're British Boys and proud of the name,*
> *Our school has always maintained its fame,*
> *Onward and upward we mean to play the game*
> *Our masters have always taught the same.*
> *Ever be British! Be British is our cry,*
> *British live and British die.*
> *We are the British, the British boys are we,*
> *We are, we are, and mean to be."*

Written by Terry Ransome

Boys' British School, Hitchin.

ム ... 九 ... (*YCLASS*   *Spring*   *Term, 192 1*

chapter 11

Queen Street School
1929 – 1969

Hertfordshire County Council took over responsibility for the running of the old British Schools in 1903; they acquired the buildings and land in 1926. And so the story changes.

After the opening of the new Wilshere-Dacre School in 1929 and the transfer of the junior classes, the infants remained at the old school. It appears that as those infants grew older and became juniors, they remained at Queen Street – possibly until room could be found for them at Wilshere-Dacre.

In 1932 the top junior class was able to move to Wilshere-Dacre, leaving only 60 children on the school rolls. However, as St Mary's school nearby was now oversubscribed, 175 pupils and 5 assistants were relocated to Queen Street, thus effectively saving Queen Street School from closure. An entry in the Infants' log book for December that year reads *"The 30 children intended for promotion are to be retained at Queen Street until midsummer, the age of promotion being raised, there being plenty of accommodation here"*.

But the problems of a large and challenging school site still remained. A school report by HMI Mr E Bloom in 1934 reads –

"The school is difficult to organise as there are two floors in one building and the hall and two classrooms are in detached buildings at the other end of the playground, but the supervision is able and the Headmistress (Mrs Harrison) has succeeded in obtaining a very happy atmosphere throughout. Good use is made of the large Hall for physical activities".

The 1930s saw the larger classrooms divided by movable screens. There were open fires surrounded with large fireguards, used to dry clothes on wet days. The Lancasterian room was known as the playroom. In it stood a piano, a gift to the school from Miss Seebohm and Mr Ransom. The playground which bordered Storehouse Lane had on one side a long open shed with wooden seats, so whatever the weather the classrooms could be vacated at break times. The gardens at the back were split into plots for the boys to work small vegetable gardens. Swimming lessons were taken at the old Queen Street baths across the road. In April 1934 a new floor was put down in the playroom. The Headmistress thought this *"a decided advantage for country dancing".*

Teachers in these years included Miss Hamilton (later to become Mrs Watts) who could terrify pupils with one icy glare. She would stay in post until 1969. Miss Whitehead became Headmistress in 1936. She was a strict teacher who stood at the top of the fire escape to ring the bell for *"In time!"* Also on the teaching staff at this time were fearsome Miss Yorke, who always kept a small cane up the long sleeve of her dress, and Mrs Topham, who arrived each morning on her motorbike and sidecar wearing a leather helmet and goggles!

1938 saw the provision of two fire extinguishers and electric lighting was installed. During the war period evacuees arrived from London (Enfield and Holborn). The school opened on Mondays, Wednesdays and Fridays for Hitchin pupils, and on Tuesdays and Thursdays for evacuees. In September 1939 the school was visited by the ARP Warden to see where trenches might be placed in the school gardens and the children were fitted for gas respirators. Gas mask parades were held regularly in the playground and ended in the classroom where the teacher tested each gas mask. The boiler room and house cellars were used as air raid shelters. A communal air raid shelter was built under St. Mary's Square, which some of the children used. With most of the young male teachers having been drafted into the armed forces, it was observed that for two terms there was not one man on the staff.

A MEMORY BY QUEEN STREET PUPIL ANGELA HILLYARD IN 'HITCHIN AT WAR'

The threat of gas bombing was real and so we had our practices in the playground, lined up as if for P.T. The drill went – (1) Gas mask out of box, (2) Put over face, (3) Make sure it fits firmly and (4) breathe normally. But I stood in the back row and pretended. Even now I can tolerate nothing over my face.

When the school reopened after the Easter holiday period in May 1940 it was again reclassified – this time as a Junior Mixed and Infants School, with 202 juniors and 117 infants. Dinner hour was actually an hour and a half, and as there was no school canteen children would either walk home or be marched down to St Mary's for a cooked lunch. September 24th 1945 saw the long awaited opening of the school canteen in the Lancasterian room with 4 kitchen staff and 2 dining room helpers.

The school uniform of the 1950s was navy and red. Mr Corbett had taken the old British School colours of royal blue and gold to Wilshere-Dacre School with him.

An ex-pupil recalls *"The three rooms to the right of the hall were the Infants' classes. All Infants had to stay to school dinners, only juniors could go home. The playground across Storehouse Lane had a lovely climbing frame. In the summer we were allowed through the gate to play on the grass. In winter the playground always iced over and we had some lovely slides on cold winter mornings. If it rained 'wet play' was sitting at your desk reading comics."*

A new reading scheme was introduced into the Infants' department in May 1952 based on Nisbet's Janet and John Books, after which the Happy Venture series were read.

A Managers' Meeting in 1956 rejected a request for the ending of the words 'British Schools' in association with Queen Street School. Celebrations took place in July 1957 – the centenary of the Girls' School building. Six months of preparation culminated in a concert at Woodside Open Air Theatre with more than half the children taking part. It was unanimously voted a success and buns and lemonade were given to everyone.

The 1960s saw the school totally overstretched and having to cope with large classes. All the staff knew that a site was being prepared in Whitehill Road for a new school and that their days at Queen Street were numbered.

As the school was bursting at

The programme for the Centenary Concert, 1957.

the seams, an extra class was opened in the Sunday School room of the old Congregational Chapel next door. Pupils walked in twos to swimming lessons in the cold outdoor baths at Butts Close on Fishponds Road. The school uniform was changed to bottle green and yellow. The navy gabardine Mac was replaced by a green one and summer school dresses were now green or yellow check. The former headmaster's house was now the staff room, P E store, office, stock room and remedial reading classroom. Caretaker Derek Baron lived in the other house. His work shed was located in the lower playground next to a 'hole-in-the-wall' boys' urinal.

In 1968 the new headmaster Nevil Richards was of the 'modern school' and set about cleansing Queen Street of ancient trappings. All cupboard doors were scrapped, which meant there could be no untidy storage areas in school. All old atlases were discarded along with the hymn books, which meant that assemblies had to be sung from typed sheets or even from memory! Lunch was eaten in the big hall and the Galleried Classroom had become the school kitchen, with ovens ranged up the steps – something of a health and safety nightmare by today's standards!

By this time there was a rich mix of children coming through the doors of the Queen Street School. There were sons and daughters of young professionals learning alongside those whose parents worked in factories. Classes were shared with recently arrived immigrant children and of course children from the traditional Hitchin stock whose ancestors had, for generations, attended the school. These were the last years for selection for the two Hitchin grammar schools and the staff coached their pupils carefully.

Whitehill School was officially opened on Wednesday 15th October 1969 by County Councillor William Hill, a former pupil of the Boys' British School. It appears that the shutting down of Queen Street School was a low-key affair – without reflection, afterthought or ceremony for such an historic and important establishment. Such apparent lack of interest in the school and its heritage seems now very surprising. Within the first few months of closure, the caretaker's shed had been burned down, windows broken and all the fire extinguishers had been set off. However, the County Council did give the buildings a reprieve when they opened the site up for adult education as an annexe of Hitchin College.

Researched and written by Jacky Birch

chapter 12

From College to Museum
1969 - 2008

In the 1970s the great Lancasterian Schoolroom was used for badminton and other leisure activities.

1969 TO 1990 - HITCHIN COLLEGE
When Hitchin College of Further Education, based in Walsworth Road, took over responsibility for the Queen Street site as its venue for adult education classes, it became known as the Queen Street Activities Centre, or QUSAC.

For 21 years, thousands of local people from North Hertfordshire's towns and villages passed through the old school's narrow gateway for 'activities'. There was a Mother and Toddler Group, a Toy Repair Workshop and practice rooms for the Hitchin Town Band.

The programme for 1981 had literally 'something for everyone' –

Indoor bowls	Dress Circle	Gardening Forum
Yoga	Toymaking	Flower Arranging
Keep Fit	Upholstery	Painting
Badminton	Lacemaking	Bridge Circle
Speech Therapy	Tailoring	Cake Decorating
Lip Reading	Soft furnishings	Antique Furniture Restoration
Disabled Persons Workshop	Dressmaking	

In June 1975, the Department of the Environment responded to a request from Jill Grey, a Hitchin resident since 1963, and it 'listed' the British Schools site as Grade 2. This was an important step – as the 'listing' procedure gives a national recognition to buildings of historical and architectural merit, and

requires special consent before any changes can be made to their fabric or layout.

Jill Grey was an avid collector of anything relating to the history of elementary education and the social history of childhood. Between 1962 and her death in 1987, she amassed some 35,000 items, most of which she kept in her own home!

In May 1977, Jill opened a private 'Museum of Education' to display just a small part of her collection in the front classroom of the 1905 wing of the Boys' School; it was later moved into the 1853 Galleried Classroom.

Her museum was only open by appointment, but about 1,000 visitors came each year. On her death in 1987, she left her large collection to North Hertfordshire District Council (NHDC) Museum Service. It was a most generous bequest, but a considerable storage problem for a Museum Service without any spare storerooms!

Mrs Jill Grey admiring the blue plaque commemorating the British Schools, which was unveiled in September 1980 by 'Old Boy' Cllr. William Hill, Chairman of Hertfordshire County Council.

1990 TO 1991 – SAVING THE SCHOOLS

The large site of historic school buildings in Queen Street was finally saved after much serious, patient and amicable negotiation between two local authorities and many individual members of the general public.

A momentous decision about its future was reached in October 1991, but to understand its significance, we must take a quick look at events of the preceding 20 months. They in turn were influenced by the people and activities on the site during the previous 21 years, 1969-1990. This familiarity with the school buildings became a springboard for sincere and generous support when the struggle began.

On 13th February 1990 a meeting was convened at Hitchin Museum to discuss the future of the Jill Grey Collection and the British Schools site. A 'Working Party' was set up, with representatives from NHDC Museum Service, Hertfordshire County Council Education and Estates Departments, the Hertfordshire Buildings Preservation Trust, and the British and Foreign Schools Society from London.

Then in May came news that the College was to leave Queen Street at the end of August – just three and a half months' notice, giving little time to determine what would happen to the site. The County Council wanted to sell it – but where could the Jill Grey Collection go? Little or no maintenance had been carried out on the school buildings since the County took them over in 1926. It was estimated that £400,000 was needed just for the urgent repairs. It was too much; the site must be sold.

In June the Working Party invited all the townspeople, children and adults alike, to tour the historic buildings, to have Sunday afternoon 'Tea and Tiffin' in the 1837 Lancasterian Teaching Hall, and to see some of the Jill Grey collection. Meanwhile Brian Limbrick, an ex pupil from the war years, had joined the Working Party. In September 1990 he enlisted the support of the education correspondents of the national newspapers, the local television stations, and BBC Radio's *Woman's Hour*. Everyone was amazed at what a 'time warp' the whole site represented. Brian appealed to the people of North Hertfordshire via the local press; he wrote in detail about the buildings and the collection, suggesting the site could become a permanent home for the Jill Grey Collection, a leisure facility for the town, and an international tourist attraction. Above all, Brian said, *"the fine old buildings are the number one priority"*. If the buildings could be saved, they would provide an ideal home for the Collection.

The Hertfordshire Buildings Preservation Trust expressed interest in collaborating with the Working Party over the ownership and restoration of the buildings. At the same time, the Department of the Environment advised that the Boys' School – including the Lancasterian schoolroom of 1837 and

Freehold for sale

OLD BRITISH SCHOOL QUEEN STREET HITCHIN

Important Grade II Listed Building with total Floor Area of approximately 10,500 SQ FT Suitable for restoration and conversion

Planning and Estates Department, County Hall, Hertford SG13 8DN (0992) 555258

Hertfordshire
COUNTY COUNCIL

Planning and Estates

"For Sale" advertisement placed by Hertfordshire County Council.

the Galleried Classroom of 1853 – had been upgraded from Grade 2 to Grade 2*, because *"the survival of these particular types of classrooms is extremely rare"*. But on 10th October the Hitchin Comet announced *"Historic Buildings are put on Market"*, followed 7 days later by *"Freehold for Sale Old British School"*. The County Council had put the site on the market – the deadline for offers was 14th December 1990. On 11th November NHDC's Arts and Culture subcommittee agreed in principle that, if and when the Working Party evolved into a charitable trust, it could be given the Jill Grey Collection.

The Working Party met at Hitchin Museum on 11th December to discuss the structure for a new charitable trust – the Hitchin British Schools Trust – and proceeded to set it up. On 14th December the Working Party made the offer to the County Council of £1 for the freehold of the premises. It was able to say that NHDC had agreed in principle to the Trust's proposals for the site, and to the donation of the Jill Grey Collection to the Trust. Everything had been done to ensure an attractive and serious bid. But, the County Council also received eight other tenders for the site.

On 1st March 1991 the County Council decided in principle to dispose of the school site to a Bedford based developer. The developer proposed conversion of the lower site to office use, and restoration of the Boys' School for community use; the company was able to bid some £200,000 for the whole site.

There was shock and disbelief among all concerned. The newspaper headlines again captured the feeling: *"Hearts Break over Hertfordshire Sale"* (*Times Educational Supplement* 8.3.91). The Trust decided to protest at this painful decision, and on 9th March, on a cold Saturday morning, shoppers throughout Hitchin's town centre were offered the chance to sign a petition of protest. By the end of the week 3,000 people had signed.

The petition was delivered to the Chairman of the County Council in Hertford in less than two weeks. Local newspapers and also the national press,

Hearts break over Hertfordshire sale

The historic "British School" at Hitchin has been sold by Hertfordshire county council to a firm of property developers despite a two-year campaign to turn the site into a working education museum.

shire education authority decided they were surplus.

The museum working party had hoped that the British School would provide a permanent home for the Jill Grey collection of

serve the buildings and the collection together as a local resource and a cultural tourist attraction for the town. It formed a trust which raised money to produce an imaginative plan for

project. It is understood that the two listed buildings will be passed on to the Jehovah's Witnesses as a meeting hall. This is likely to satisfy the planning requirement for community use.

including *The Guardian* and *The Times Educational Supplement*, all wrote detailed articles and published letters in support of the Trust's proposals. The Trust was not to be beaten. It engaged a property consultant to act on its behalf in negotiations with the County Council. And there was good news when, in May 1991, the District Council approved plans for the site to become a museum. Four months after its original decision, the County Council expressed a willingness to reconsider. NHDC supported the Trust's proposals with enthusiasm, and argued with the County Council that the purchase figure for the site should not be based on its supposed commercial value.

The Trust and its advisers gave a presentation to three County Councillors and their officers in the Lancasterian schoolroom on a chilly and very wet morning in July 1991. During the discussions, a new leak opened up in the roof and rain water poured in; no comments were made while the buckets were moved into position! The County Councillors announced they wished to discuss the proposed course of action with NHDC.

In late September, at a meeting of the full Council, NHDC agreed to pledge £205,000 by way of loan or guarantee to support the purchase of the Queen Street site by the Trust. Cllr Bob Flatman commented *"We hope that this will encourage the County Council to sell the school to the Trust. Our action has certainly made the Trust's offer more attractive."* Following NHDC's offer, further discussions took place between the Trust and the County Council, and finally, in October, a local newspaper was able to announce – *"School Battlers Celebrate"* (*The Comet* 9.10.91)

School Battlers Celebrate

CAMPAIGNERS who fought to save part of Hit-chin's heritage are cele-brating after winning their battle.

They have persuaded Herts County Council to sell them the historic British Schools site in Queen Street rather than to de-velopers.

The chase price of around £200,000, the county council has decided to sell the site to the British Schools Trust.

Trust director and vice-chairman Brian Limbrick said this week: "We are walking on Cloud Nine."

Bryan Smalley, vice-chairman of the county council's policy operation sub-committee and spokesman said: "Both the County property matters and that of the rick Upton scheme and imaginative schemes which trust were met the principal requirement.

1991 TO 2008 – LEARNING COMES TO LIFE – AGAIN

It was a new beginning. But it was not to be until January 1994 that the Trust eventually took legal possession of the site.

The first task, and one that took many volunteers and many months, was to clean up the site and to make it safe for visitors. The historic buildings had lain empty for some time and had deteriorated further.

Visitors came, slowly at first, escorted around the site by members of the Trust. By 1996 parts of the Schools were opened to the first 'proper' visitors – members of the public and organised school classes. However, the opening of the great Lancasterian Schoolroom to visitors had to be delayed until 1998 – regrettably, the ceiling had to be removed for fear that it would collapse.

Progress continued. In 2002 the British Schools became a Registered Museum, and in 2003 the site was honoured by a Royal Visit, from His Royal Highness the Duke of Gloucester, a supporter of museums and galleries. In 2006 the Headmaster's house was opened to the public, having been renovated and furnished to create a home such as Mr Fitch and his family might have enjoyed in the 1890s.

The British Schools have been well and truly 'saved'. But the struggle continues to restore and preserve them for future generations to use and appreciate.

Researched and written by Elizabeth Hunter

Acknowledgements

T he authors thank all those who gave so freely of their time and
expertise in the preparation of this book. Firstly, however, this project
could not have gone ahead without a generous Local Heritage
Initiative grant from the Heritage Lottery Fund. We are truly grateful for this
opportunity and wish to thank Sylvia Collier, HLF Senior Grants Officer, for
her help and advice.

For information, our first points of reference were the records and notes
held in the British Schools Museum Collection. Curator Fiona Dodwell was
always helpful in providing access to the documents held there, many of
which had been collected by the late Mrs Jill Grey. Much more information
had been gathered by museum volunteers, in particular by Brian and
Yvonne Limbrick whose knowledge of the site and its history proved
invaluable.

However, there were many gaps and unanswered questions in our
knowledge. The more we looked, the more we realised that in order to
publish the story of the Masters much more research was needed.

The internet – not readily available in 1990 when the museum was being
founded – proved an invaluable source of knowledge and inspiration.

Visits to the British and Foreign School Society archives at Brunel
University's Runnymede campus at Egham, Surrey, were a revelation to us.
Nothing was too much trouble for curator Helen Betteridge who identified
and retrieved original documents and correspondence for us – providing us
with much new material. Bridget Howlett at the London Metropolitan
Archive also deserves our thanks.

We paid several fruitful visits to Hertfordshire Archives and Local
Studies, and are grateful to staff for their advice, assistance and helpful
suggestions, in particular to Dr Jill Barber, Heritage Services Manager, and
Sue Flood, County Archivist. We were also welcomed to the Hertfordshire
County Council Legal and Estates Department Archive by Barbara Jones,
Registry Supervisor.

John and Janet Pearson of the Hertfordshire Family History Society
gave specialist genealogical advice. Carole Casey of North Hertfordshire
District Council helped us with the location of burial plots.

Curator David Hodges, Assistant Curator Jenny Oxley and their staff at
Hitchin Museum gave us valuable help; generally, in enabling us to build a
picture of early educational opportunities in the town, and specifically by

allowing frequent access to the valuable British Schools archive material in their care. Staff at Hitchin Library enabled us to study the entries in the St Mary's Parish Church registers.

Patricia C O'Donnell from The Society of Friends' Historical Library at Swarthmore College, Pennsylvania helped us with new information regarding Joseph Lancaster's death and burial.

All of these organisations kindly provided digital images and gave us permission to publish the material.

Editorial and publication guidance was given by Priscilla Douglas and Pauline Humphries of Hitchin Historical Society and by Barrie Dack.

Memories, ephemera and specialist knowledge give life to a project such as this. We sincerely thank the following for their information, suggestions and enthusiasm: Joan Abbiss, Wendy Cant, Cheryl Catlin, Vivien Cook, Joan Cullen and Michael Brockett, Lance Dimsey, Joyce Donald, Ann Fitch, Jean Handley, Angela Hillyard, Andy Leigh, Hilary Merritt, Jane Smyth, Linley Walker and Derek Wheeler.

Artistic input was provided by Daphne Gibson. Photography was in the capable hands of Colin Hewett of Hitchin Camera Club, and Ruth Cannon.

Sheila Graham, Mel Knights, Brian and Yvonne Limbrick, and Ralph Westell all read the book in its early stages and made valuable comments or gave useful advice. Simon Walker kindly advised us on indexing.

The onerous task of proofreading was taken on by Fiona Dodwell, Bridget Howlett, Mel Knights, Leslie Mustoe and Derek Wheeler.

Finally, the magical transition from CD to book was performed by Chris Murray.

Any errors or omissions are, however, entirely our own.

Picture Acknowledgements

All photographs and illustrations other than those listed below are part of the British Schools Museum Collection.

We are grateful to the following for permission to use their images –

The British and Foreign School Society: p8/9, p43, p47, p52, p58, p62
The British Library: p15 © British Library Board. All Rights Reserved. Shelf mark 1387.d.10
City of London, London Metropolitan Archives: p13
Hertfordshire Archives and Local Studies: p33 bottom ref. DES1/43, p45 ref. 58875, p56/57, p68 and p69 ref. DES1/43. All reproduced by kind permission of Hertfordshire Archives and Local Studies
Hitchin Museum: p20, p26, p29, p30, p33 top, p34, p53, p63, p64, p65, p71, p86, p91, p101, p109, p111, p117
National Portrait Gallery, London: p17

Our thanks also go to the following volunteers and friends of the British Schools Museum for providing photographs, images and sketches –

Joan Abbiss: p95 top, **Ruth Cannon:** pvi, p2, p24, **Wendy Cant:** p113, **Rick Dodwell:** p119, **Priscilla Douglas:** p87, **Ann Fitch:** p85, p88, p94, **Daphne Gibson:** p48, p92, p102, **Colin Hewett of Hitchin Camera Club**: inside front and back covers (lower images), **Rosemary Ransome:** p95 bottom, **Linley Walker:** p36.

Sources

BRITISH SCHOOLS MUSEUM, QUEEN STREET, HITCHIN
- Aitken E.R. *Queen Street Centenary Celebrations – a brief history.* Leaflet, 1957
- Limbrick B. *William John Fitch 1826–1902, The Master of Hitchin.* Unpublished manuscript, 2004
- Lopez-Portillo y Lancaster-Jones R.A. Copies of written papers on Joseph Lancaster, and personal correspondence
- Hitchin Boys' British School Log Books 1863–1900
- Relevant papers and material in the Jill Grey Collection

HITCHIN MUSEUM, PAYNES PARK, HITCHIN
- Lawson Thompson Scrapbooks, Loftus Barham Scrapbooks, Militia Lists, Hertfordshire Express Newspaper Archive, Hitchin Schools Archive boxes
- Aitken E.R. *The Development of Education in Hitchin 1780 – 1880.* MA thesis for University of Nottingham, 1960
- Dunnage W. History of Hitchin. Unpublished manuscript, 1815
- Lucas F. Hitchin Biography, 1875
- Commonplace Book of William Wilshere, 1814
- Hitchin British Schools Boys' Evening School Account Book (John Ransom, Treasurer) 1812 - 1818
- Hitchin British Schools Trustees' Minute Books
- Hitchin British Boys' School Log Book 1900–1929

HERTFORDSHIRE ARCHIVES AND LOCAL STUDIES, COUNTY HALL, HERTFORD
- British Directory 1794
- Account Books of 1811 & 1822 (William Wilshere Collection)
- Letters (William Wilshere Collection)
- Minutes of Property Book of 1811 (William Wilshere Collection)
- Rental Books of 1816 & 1822 (William Wilshere Collection)
- Queen Street Congregational Church Book No.1, 1715–1822
- Builders' and Architects' plans for the Hitchin British School, 1853 and 1857
- Map of Hitchin by J Bailey Denton, 1844

THE BRITISH & FOREIGN SCHOOL SOCIETY ARCHIVE, BRUNEL UNIVERSITY, EGHAM, SURREY

❑ Bartle George F. *The role of the BFSS in the Country Towns of S.E. England during the 19th Century* in History of Education Society Bulletin, No. 56 Autumn 1995

❑ Collins G. Introduction to *A Transcription of letters written by Joseph Lancaster between 6th November 1810 and April 21st 1812*

❑ Lancaster J. *Improvements in Education 1803* (Facsimile Edition), BFSS, 1998

❑ Lancaster J. *Seven pamphlets, 1806–1811* (Facsimile Edition), Unifacmanu Trading Co Ltd, 1995

❑ Salmon D. *A Retrospect: Lancaster as Lecturer,* BFSS Educational Record Vol.16 Feb.1902 – Oct.1905

❑ Report of the Royal Lancasterian Institution 1811

❑ Testimonial files – Queen's Scholarship applicants

❑ Correspondence files – British Schools to the BFSS

PRINTED SOURCES

❑ Adamson J.W. *A Short History of Education*, Cambridge University Press, 1922

❑ Agar N. *Hitchin's Straw Plait Industry,* Hitchin Historical Society / North Hertfordshire District Council, 1982

❑ Armytage W.H.G. *Four Hundred Years of English Education*, Cambridge University Press, 1970

❑ Bartle G.F. *A History of Borough Road College*, Bartle, 1976

❑ Brittany A. *Hats off to the past, Coats off to the future* (A history of Wilshere-Dacre School), One Bee Books, 1997

❑ Castleden Rodney *British History,* Parragon, 1994

❑ Corston W. *A Brief Sketch of the Life of Joseph Lancaster*, c1840

❑ Crosby T. et al *Jeeves' Yard, A Dynasty of Hitchin Builders and Brickmakers,* Street Publishers, Baldock, 2003

❑ Curtis S.J. *History of Education in Great Britain*, University Tutorial Press, 1965

❑ Curtis S.J. & Boultwood M.E. *An Introductory History of English Education since 1800*, University Tutorial Press, 1966

❑ Dodwell F. *Hitchin British Schools, A History of the Buildings,* The Friends of The Hitchin British Schools Museum, 1994

❑ Dodwell F. *Hitchin British Schools Schooldays 1810–1900,* North Hertfordshire District Council, 1993

❑ Donald J. *The John Mattocke Boys,* (A History of the Hitchin Boys' Grammar School), Donald, 1990

❏ Douglas P. and Humphries P. *The House that Bartlett Built,*
Hitchin Historical Society and Hitchin Forum, 1996
❏ Edwards H.C. and Moles B.A. *Wilshere-Dacre 1929–1979,*
The Hive Printers, 1979
❏ Fisher G. *The Instructor or Young Man's Best Companion,*
A. Bettesworth & C. Hitch, 1794
❏ Fitzpatrick S. & West B. *The Street Names of Hitchin and their Origins: Book 1,
The Town Centre,* Egon Publishers Ltd, 1996
❏ Foster A.M. (Ed. Munby L.M.) *Market Town,* Hitchin Historical Society, 1987
❏ Hamel J. *Der Gegenseitige Unterricht; Geschichte seiner Einführung und
Ausbreitung durch Dr. A. Bell, J. Lancaster und andere;…..,* Paris, 1818
❏ *Hertfordshire Burial Index 1800–1851,*
Hertfordshire Family History Society, 2005
❏ Hine R.L. *Hitchin Worthies,* George Allen & Unwin, 1932
❏ Hine R.L. *Relics of an Un-Common Attorney,* John Dent & Sons Ltd, 1951
❏ Hine R.L. *The History of Hitchin Vol.II,* George Allen & Unwin Ltd, 1929
❏ Hodges D. and Ransome T. (Eds.) *Hitchin at War,*
North Hertfordshire District Council & Hitchin British Schools Trust, 2005
❏ Horn P. *The Victorian and Edwardian Schoolchild,* Sutton, 1989
❏ Hurt J.S. *Bringing Literacy to Rural England,* Phillimore & Co Ltd, 1972
❏ Jones M.G. *The Charity School Movement,* Cambridge University Press, 1938
❏ Lopez-Portillo R.A. *Lancasterian Education in Mexico,* in Update Mexico, 1998
❏ Lucas W. *A Quaker Journal,* Ed. Bryant G.E & Baker G.P., Hutchinson & Co, 1934
❏ Pieris M. *Take 6 carrots….. The recipes of a Hertfordshire Family,*
Hitchin Historical Society, 1994
❏ Taylor J. *Joseph Lancaster: The Poor Child's Friend,* The Campanile Press, 1996
❏ Urwick W. *Non-Conformity in Hertfordshire,* Hazell Watson & Viney, 1884
❏ Walmsley R. *Early Education in Hitchin,* (new edition)
Hitchin Historical Society, 1998
❏ West E.G. *Education and Crime: A Political Economy of Independence,*
Character, Vol. 8, No. 4 June 1980

OTHER SOURCES
❏ Hitchin Library – Census 1801, 1841, 1851, 1861, 1871 1881, 1891, 1901
❏ Hitchin Library – St Mary's Church marriage records 1811
❏ North Hertfordshire District Council, Letchworth –
Burial records for St John's Road Cemetery, Hitchin
❏ Swarthmore College, Swarthmore, Pennsylvania, USA –
Society of Friends' Burial Records
❏ Ancestry.co.uk (Family History, census information)
❏ The Worldwide Web (Timeline, general research and census searches)

Index

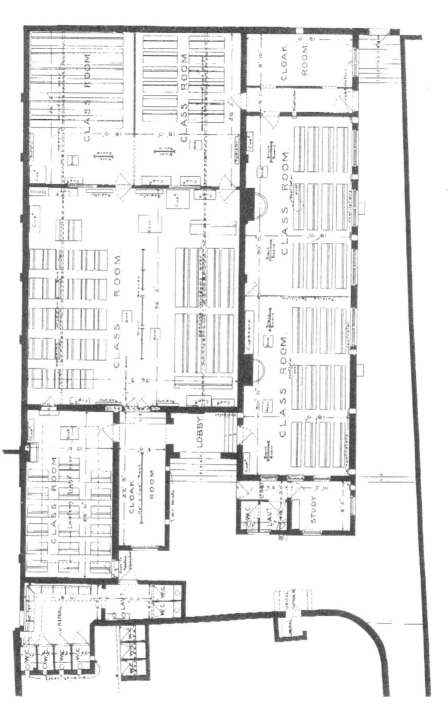

The plan of the Boys' School for 1914 shows a very crowded layout.